The Politics of Communication

THE POLITICS OF COMMUNICATION

*A Study in the Political Sociology of
Language, Socialization, and Legitimation*

CLAUS MUELLER

OXFORD UNIVERSITY PRESS
London   Oxford   New York

OXFORD UNIVERSITY PRESS

London   Oxford   New York
Glasgow   Toronto   Melbourne   Wellington
Cape Town   Ibadan   Nairobi   Dar es Salaam   Lusaka   Addis Ababa
Delhi   Bombay   Calcutta   Madras   Karachi   Lahore   Dacca
Kuala Lumpur   Singapore   Hong Kong   Tokyo

für michael bau, freund und begleiter,
28 september 1941–16 februar 1969

notre vie est un voyage.
dans l'hiver et dans la nuit
nous cherchons notre passage
dans le ciel
ou rien ne luit

PREFACE

The reader who expects solutions to contemporary political problems will not be satisfied with this book nor will those oriented to theoretical expositions. There is little material in these pages that supports political fatalism or revolutionary rhetoric. What I have attempted to do is to provide an empirically grounded analysis of advanced industrial society and of those problems that appear unsurmountable within the established institutional context.

This analysis relates factors that have appeared unrelated heretofore. Certainly, there is literature in the field of political socialization, communication, and, as of late, legitimation. But most works do not tie these phenomena to each other or to the structure of advanced capitalist society. Political phenomena do not exist in isolation. The question of loyalty to a political system, for example, touches upon factors that are more refined than those forming the standard stock of the social sciences. Concepts such as plausibility structures, socialization strategies, language codes, ideological configurations, political impression management, and legitimating and counterlegitimating rationales provide a better grasp of political behavior and its underlying motivational basis than an analysis that restricts itself to the usual factors like education, occupation, and religion.

The approach chosen here has its disadvantages. There are gaps in the course of the argument; speculations interlace the text; and frequent incursions into areas that are not my domain are made. However, the nature of the political system in advanced industrial society in general and in the United States in particular has set new parameters for scientific analysis and political action. They render obsolete a number of theoretical and common sense notions about political conflict and change. A rapidly changing class structure, the reassertion of the political realm as embodied in the growing autonomy of the state, the slow movement toward a benevolent but authoritarian state, and the concomittant delegitimation of political authority pose new questions that require inquiries unhampered by inherited paradigms.

A constant dialogue with friends and colleagues accompanied work on the book over the last years. Neither Peter Berger, Pierre Bourdieu, nor Jürgen Habermas will agree with all of the ideas advanced here; the book nevertheless profited greatly from their encouragement and criticism as it did from discussions with Peter Dreitzel, Urs Jaeggi, Claus Offe, Philipp Weintraub, and Angela-Francesca Zanotti Karp. There is no question that the quality of the book was improved by the broad editorial assistance of Carol Coe Conway which frequently helped to clarify further the basic argument of the book and served to eliminate much of the sociological jargon that pervaded the first drafts of the manuscript.

My appreciation goes to Manuela Kruger, Harriet Serenkin, Anne M. Jones, Ilene Greenfield, and all those at Oxford University Press and Hunter College who were of great help to a restless and sometimes idiosyncratic author.

I am happy that less than two years after the publication of the hard cover edition, English and German paperbacks are in print making this book available to a larger public. With the exception of few revised passages and statistics and minor bibliographical corrections, this edition is identical to the hard cover version.

June Farm
Towers, New York
July 1973
February 1975

CONTENTS

The Politics of Communication

INTRODUCTION

The eruption of large-scale civil disorders, marked by the spread of student radicalism, civil disobedience, and political violence in the late sixties, shattered the belief of many observers that the stability of social and political institutions and the peaceful integration of minority groups into the mainstream of American society were representative features of this country.

The active or passive acceptance of political institutions and societal goals by the majority of the population had been reflected in the terminology of social scientists and journalists. "Integration" of individuals and groups into the political order, "consensus" regarding the goals of society, and "adaptation" to existing institutions were standard terms for the analysis of American society, which appeared (or was made to appear) a politically balanced one. Books written from widely differing perspectives affirmed the stability of the sociopolitical arrangements. For Herbert Marcuse, society and man had become one dimensional.[1] In his view, coercion and repression were no longer explanations for political domination, and he argued that large segments of the population had become integrated since their language and consciousness were such that they no longer conceived of ideas and values that contradicted the established political order. For Daniel Bell, the "end of ideology" had come and, implicitly, the end of major societal conflicts.[2] Pluralism appeared to many as a working feature of the political system which allowed for at least minimal fulfillment of the needs of all groups in society.[3] Arnold Rose tried to demonstrate that there were indeed countervailing powers and institutions which offset the influence of the power elite described by C. Wright Mills.[4] Others proposed that attitudes and values supportive of political institutions had been successfully transmitted in the socialization process.[5]

From both Marcusian and strictly behaviorist perspectives, similarities between the interpretations of political reality by those in power and by those subjected to it could be extrapolated. Politics, as the ongoing discussion of means and ends, seemed to subside since what was meaningful for the rulers appeared to be meaningful for the ruled as well. Neither view could account for the creation of alternative political values since the methods of investigation excluded a consideration of human communication as a basis for new political interpretations.

Interaction between citizens and their government appeared to be a programmed process and the direction of social change a linear one since goals were predefined by established institutions and sustained by vested interests. These integration models implied, moreover, that individuals and groups in society were no longer able to decode or understand the contradictions and conflicts of the political environment and were therefore prevented from acting on them. The individual living in advanced industrial society apparently identified himself with the existing political structures and goals by accepting them without question as his own.[6]

The above views had some plausibility. There were indications of a reduction of conflicts linked to political ideologies which traditionally provided the basis for conflicting symbols and visions. Neither socialism nor liberalism seemed to offer an ideology through which opposition to the technocratic rationale of highly industrial societies could be articulated. Underpinning the above views were the supportive political attitudes of the working and lower-middle classes, particularly in the United States.

In the late sixties, however, the language of observers and analysts slowly changed to incorporate concepts and arguments which made it clear that "integration" and "consensus" did not suffice to explain either the apparent structural crisis or the politics of dissent. Terms such as "discontinuity" (unexpected ruptures in institutional or political development), "anomie" (the absence of norms and standards), and "counterculture" entered the discussion. Daniel Moynihan summarized what he termed the "erosion of authority of the institutions of American society." Early in 1969 he stated in a memorandum to the President of the United States that "what is at issue is the continued acceptance by the great mass of the people of the legitimacy and efficacy of the present arrangements of American society and of our processes for changing those arrangements." [7]

The process of delegitimation, implied by Moynihan, renders the use of the term "political integration" somehow suspect. Nevertheless, that concept serves as a point of departure for analyzing the loyalty a political order enjoys. Present-day capitalist societies are certainly not completely integrated, but neither are they in a state of anarchy, beset by ethnic groups and social classes that wage war on each other or on governmental institutions. The question arises as to what are the factors which constitute the basis of legitimacy and political integration.

Talleyrand is said to have made the observation that one can do many things with a sword, except sit on it. He was referring to the impossibility of a political system maintaining itself over a long period of time by violently repressing dissenting factions. Rather, it is generally argued that authority is upheld by the belief that the exercise of power is legitimate.[8] It has been suggested that the voluntary submission of man to political institutions is contingent on reduced individuation[9] and that the establishment of a political community depends on the existence of leaders who provide values that are successfully universalized.[10] Censorship and directed communication, understood as overt means to control language and communication, are conspicuous methods of universalizing values and manipulating consciousness to thereby prevent corrosion of a system's legitimacy by counter symbols and values. An analysis of these means and of dominant values does not, however, suffice to explain why most strata have been integrated into the political order. Even in modern societies characterized by the selective release and publication of information and the dilution of public communication through the mass media, the integrating factors are located on a different level.

The *typical idea* of an integrated society is one in which political, social, and economic needs that groups experience and articulate can be anticipated and fulfilled by the established institutions. The belief in the legitimacy of the political order depends, therefore, on (1) the satisfaction of articulated needs and (2) the transmission and regeneration of values which permit a minimal degree of solidarity among the members of a political community.

In order to see the limits of political integration in advanced capitalist societies, it is necessary to analyze sources of stability and instability alike. Insofar as sources of stability are concerned, it is significant that although the dissent and rebellion of the late sixties drew substantial support from the more privileged strata in society, the overwhelming majority of the population remained, for the most part, silent and loyal to the "establishment." Obviously, there has been organized dissent as well as the spontaneous and sometimes violent dissent of segments of deprived minority groups. But the political status and the economic position of these groups in the process of production are marginal and render them secondary in an analysis of system stability.[11] By themselves, these groups are not in a position, politically speaking, to enforce their demands. Only demands made by groups whose withdrawal of cooperation endangers economic growth have to be taken seriously. The support and cooperation of the working and middle classes are strategically more important for the American political order than that of groups which approximate what Karl Marx called the *Lumpenproletariat*. The political status of the underprivileged and the loyalty of blue- and white-collar workers to political institutions make both groups unlikely candidates for effective opposition.

Another reason for stability is that in advanced capitalist society catastrophic visions based on the inevitability of economic crises are no longer credible. Significant changes in the political system over the last decades have made it possible for the state to increase its control over a number of factors which previously caused instability. In the past, instability in capitalist societies resulted from conflicts between groups and classes, from the incapacity of the nation-state to provide vital services to the population, or more frequently, from cyclical depressions of the economy.

In recent decades, antagonism between groups and classes waned because each profited, more or less, from the economic growth of the postwar period. The industrial expansion of Western powers has permitted the satisfaction of material needs of both working and middle classes. This expansion allowed for the political acceptance of demands for increases in the standard of living.[12] A steadily growing consumption of goods and services, necessary for an expanding economy, is encouraged by a consumer ideology which is seemingly not questioned by the great majority of people. The assumption that present and future material needs can be met appears plausible since demands for greater quantitative compensations, such as higher wages and more leisure time, do not pose an insurmountable challenge for an advanced industrial society. Thus the stability of the political order appears assured if the primary or consumer needs of groups, whose cooperation is necessary for further economic growth, are satisfied.

Institutional stability was also buttressed by the ever-growing control of the executive branch of governments over the decision-making process. Because of an open or hidden transfer of decision-making power away from representative bodies, the power of presidents and prime ministers has burgeoned. At the same time, the autonomy of political divisions of both national states and local communities has diminished as they have become increasingly dependent on national resources and authorities. Executive offices have become "steering centers" which are relatively independent of other institutions such as elected assemblies and political parties which traditionally arbitrated the demands of interest groups and governments.

The shift of power to the top was accompanied by an increased regulation of society and its economy by national governments which today provide welfare to a steadily growing number of clients, be they underprivileged minority groups or large corporations. Given the economic dependence of large segments of the population and institutional sectors on it, the state is structurally constrained to intervene in order to ensure economic and political stability.

The satisfaction of material needs of the greater part of the population, sufficient control of economic development, and the predominance of executive power have stabilized capitalist societies. But at the same time new sources of instability have become apparent. They appear to be located in the incapacity of societies to fulfill newly emerging qualitative needs and demands. Qualitative or ideal needs, such as the quest for self-fulfillment and new political and social values, cannot be satisfied by quantitative compensations. The questioning of consumer and achievement ideologies can neither be transformed into marketable commodities nor subject to effective sanctions. A demand such as participatory democracy reflects an individual's need to have a say in those decisions that affect his life. Because this need is not alien to generally held values, if it goes unfulfilled it undermines the claim to legitimacy of the political system.

Any demand that cannot be met within the logic of the system and its established priorities, that requires a redistribution of power, or that jeopardizes the fundamental condition for economic stability, namely, perpetual expansion, must be excluded. The regulation of society from above, with the expressed goal of preserving and stabilizing existing sociopolitical arrangements, requires the suppression or control of group needs which cannot be satisfied institutionally.[13] The quest for "community control" over national antipoverty funds, for instance, runs counter to the presumed rational administration of these funds from above and undercuts welfare as a means to control the poor.[14]

These qualitative or ideal needs, which emanate from and express values contrary to official ones, cannot be articulated through the traditional trade union ideology since for pragmatic reasons, that ideology has been adjusted to material needs and demands. Nor can pluralism serve as a reference point since it is basically a bargaining matrix for the distribution of material goods and services. Strangely enough, value orientations which are not strictly political in character, be they humanistic or religious, can serve as the background for the articulation of qualitative needs which, once manifested politically, lose their abstract character. For example, the ideal of equality for all men and women, if restricted to the future, is no political problem. Demanded for the present, it spells conflict in any society based on social inequality.

The locus of potential instability has thus shifted from the economic base to values and beliefs, although the latter are not completely disconnected from the former. The key problem is no longer the avoidance of depressions since they can be checked, rather it is the maintenance and sustenance of the loyalties of the population which will demonstrate that "the existing political institutions are the most appropriate ones for the society." [15] The key issue could be subsumed under the term "value crisis management," in other words, effective political socialization and conditioning of society.

This study attempts to show that the phenomenon of political integration applies primarily to those groups that cannot articulate their interests or perceive societal conflicts. Since they have been socialized into compliance, so to speak, they accept the definitions of political reality as offered by dominant groups, classes, and governmental institutions. While arguing that the prevalence of economic interests[16] (be they linked to official policies or not) has caused a growing gap between the social and industrial sectors of advanced capitalist societies, it will be shown that potential conflict zones have shifted from the lower to the middle classes. It is within the latter groups, whose allegiance to the American political order was once a given, that today one can observe anomic tendencies, that is, the breakdown of loyalties tying them to established institutions and the values of society at large.

The absence of an integrating political ideology provides a possible but limited explanation for the erosion of loyalties and authority. This erosion, or what will be called here *the process of delegitimation*, is the second focal point of this study. Neither a pure functionalist nor a pure Marxist approach proves itself alone sufficient for the analysis of the phenomena underlying the delegitimation of political institutions and traditional value structures. A combination of concepts derived from both schools permits the recovery of two factors which have a major impact on the individual's political consciousness: linguistic ability and socialization patterns or methods of child rearing through which the individual is molded into a member of society. Since variations in both language and socialization are specific to social classes, an analysis of these factors and their link to legitimating and delegitimating processes cannot be disconnected from class structure. This analysis, though limited to advanced capitalist societies, lends itself to certain extrapolations for industrialized communist societies.*

* This study and the related empirical material covers the United States, Great Britain, France, and West Germany. The American situation is stressed since both the integration of the working class and the alienation of segments of the middle class are more evident here than in Europe. There are a number of basic similarities between advanced capitalist and socialist societies, such as the emphasis on economic expansion and science and technology. Consumerism is also becoming a feature of advanced socialist societies. There is not much empirical evidence available on class-specific socialization patterns and language codes in socialist societies, but indirect evidence (e.g., class-specific educational success and social background of elite groups) indicates that these variables may play a role in socialist societies too. Insofar as the social basis of dissent is concerned, it is interesting to note that the unrest

The connection between socialization and language, on one hand, and legitimating and delegitimating processes, on the other, has not been analyzed to date by political sociologists, nor has the process of delegitimation proper been a major focus of interest since prevailing interpretations have posited legitimacy as an a priori factor,[17] locating sources of potential instability among conflicting group interests or the dynamics of economic development. It appears, however, that the particular constellation of economic, social, and political factors noted above renders advanced capitalist societies vulnerable or "soft" at a point which hitherto appeared secure: the transmission from one generation to the next of values and socially and politically motivating symbols which induce acceptance of authority.

Class-specific socialization patterns and linguistic codes decisively influence the way in which individuals relate to institutionalized authority. It will be argued that the political symbols and the structure of the language of the middle classes, specifically of the group Richard Flacks called the "humanistic subculture," [18] and the flexible socialization patterns of that stratum create the preconditions for dissent and for the generation of values that contradict dominant ones. In short, language and socialization mediate the success of a political system's claim to legitimacy.

Cognitive capacities and political values are important variables in this discussion.[19] An adequate understanding of politics presupposes the ability to discern the political nature of problems that are disguised as individual or technical ones. The problem of pollution, for example, though frequently presented as a tech-

---

which East Germany experienced in 1954 and Poland in 1970 was linked to material deprivations of the working class, whereas the uprising in Hungary in 1956 and Dubček's short-lived government in the CSSR of 1968 were based primarily on political demands such as the redistribution of authority and the removal of censorship and restrictions on personal freedom. These latter demands were articulated essentially by segments of the upper-middle class. Advanced socialist societies differ, however, from advanced capitalist ones in that the integrating ideology and the legitimacy of existing institutions in these societies has not eroded to the extent that the term delegitimation would be justified.

nical issue, is related to political structures and requires a governmental response. The existence of an elaborated language with its implicit decoding facilities and the prevalence of flexible socialization patterns constitute preconditions for the alienation and repoliticization of segments of the middle classes. Conversely, vast segments of the population are integrated into the political order because their capacity to engage rationally and symbolically in public discourse is severely limited by their linguistic environments. In addition to its potential for dissent, language becomes significant politically, because, if restricted, it makes the perception and articulation of needs virtually impossible. The existence of distorted communication which obscures, filters, and splits the universe of subjective and collective understanding will be demonstrated on the societal and individual levels in order to show the sociopolitical functions of language.

1

DISTORTED COMMUNICATION

THE ROLE OF LANGUAGE

Man's capacity to form symbols and words which represent phenomena of his external and internal worlds is his most distinguishing characteristic. In the process of discerning and decoding his environment, man creates symbolic systems or languages which structure and transform it. Words provide molds for concepts and thoughts, as well as for symbols that reflect beliefs and values. Unlike a sign which can be reduced to a fixed content such as a number, symbols and concepts have an open semantic space delimited only by interpretations. The nature and function of language cannot, however, be disconnected from the social realm.

Language provides the opportunity for engaging in social interaction and serves as the main agent of man's integration into a culture, an integration which an individual or group cannot oppose since there is no choice but to acquire the language of the culture into which one happens to be born. Jointly shared symbolic expressions which are articulated through language are the means of socialization and create a social bond between individuals and groups since the roles and social relations available in society are transmitted and internalized through language.[1] As Julius

Lafall has noted, language conditions the individual to cultural patterns; it is "an instrument of interpersonal behavior and . . . essentially a means of incorporating the individual into an existing cultural matrix and of guaranteeing his contribution to the needs and aspirations of the culture." [2] It allows for a communion between the individual and his group and establishes a link between the self and others.

Language also provides the basis for self-reflection and individuation because it enables the individual to reason with himself and preserve, through a dialogue with himself and others, those aspects which set him apart from others. The self can be grasped in "the mirror of its own expression and become the object of the inner view" only through one's own speech.[3]

It would be a mistake, however, to assume that there exists a uniform cultural matrix for any society. In other words, although there are codifications of languages as formulated in grammars and dictionaries, the standard language of a society is not internalized by all members to the same extent. Obviously, they all learn the same language,* but linguistic variations come into play which go beyond those of dialect and diction and which are a reflection of socioeconomic conditions. Linguistic codes have come into existence which differentiate ethnic groups and social classes from one another and from the rest of society. The code of a group reflects the socioeconomic conditions of that group, while the environment, in turn, reinforces and validates the individual's language. In the process of acquiring words, concepts, symbols, and syntactic structures, the individual confirms his knowledge and language by testing them against his environment. As a result, he unintentionally assimilates the political and social values or reference dimensions of his group. Language, then, or more precisely the code a group shares, is context specific. The

* Exceptions are provided by minority groups speaking a foreign language. It is reasonable to assume nonetheless that a Puerto Rican, for example, when he comes to speak English, will do so in a manner which reflects both his social and educational status.

possibility of transcending the content of one's code is contingent upon accepting and learning other codes. Change from one code to another implies, therefore, not only a change of the language spoken but also a change of the social context.

Whether one accepts Noam Chomsky's conception of innate mental structures as the determining influence on linguistic development or Jean Piaget's theory of the decisive role of actions in cognitive growth, language acquisition and development cannot be disconnected from the environment.[4] Concepts and perceptions are reinforced by stimuli and responses from the environment, even if "the development of perceptual and conceptual organization . . . antedates the development of speech."[5]

Man's existence is made possible by his capacity to express symbolically his responses to the physical and social environment. The symbolic and conceptual interpretations embedded in his acquired language become, however, a mediating factor that shapes his view of the environment. Language is a repository of cultural tradition, and changes the individual makes in his language are minimal, unless he switches from one subcode to another or his language is manipulated.

Man can be conscious of something if he knows a name for it and if he can place it within his linguistic and conceptual framework. Language can thus be understood as a necessary precondition for thought since it provides the building stones for thought processes. Only when thoughts and concepts are expressed through language do they exist. Certainly, there are phenomena and sentiments that do not require words to be communicated, but such communication remains diffuse until words are attached to it. New words and concepts are created if changes in the environment come about which require new symbolic interpretations. But even when this occurs, a new concept, be it a new term or the redefinition of an old term, cannot be disconnected from the cultural or linguistic heritage. Paul Chauchard thus writes, "all education and the development of the power of abstraction and of reason are only a perfection of language and its written manifesta-tions." * [6]

Thought and perception are influenced by language in several ways. Words and concepts at one's disposal make information (or stimuli) coming from the environment comprehensible. Informa-tion cannot be adequately perceived or decoded if the terms and categories, by means of which the decoding process takes place, are not available. There is evidence from ethnographic research which indicates that a high level of categorial differentiation re-sults in sharper perception. Data reveal that the ability to classify plants and to discriminate colors is frequently a function of lin-guistic factors. It is, for instance, well known that Eskimos know how to distinguish between more than a dozen different types of snow because their language makes this codification possible. Fur-thermore, the mere knowledge of words can affect our reasoning. Experiments have been made which demonstrate that the ignor-ance of terms or categories that are instrumental for solving an experimental problem influences the outcome of the experiment. Subjects who have stored certain terms in their minds are more likely to succeed in solving a problem than those who have not.[7]

Metaphorically, language and the concepts and words embedded in it are posed between the individual and his environment and serve as an invisible filter. The individual attains a certain degree of understanding through the classification made possible by concepts that screen and structure perception. The number and quality of concepts available to the individual allow him to or-ganize information and experiences. This process of mediation is not necessarily a conscious one since the language one speaks and the concepts one masters are taken for granted and are not ex-perienced as a reality of their own. An individual who under-stands (or labels) education, for example, as vocational training only, will not be aware of the nonutilitarian benefits of his schooling.

* All translations from French or German texts are the author's, unless other-wise indicated.

On a more abstract level, a similar mechanism comes into play. If concepts can be related one to another, it is possible to reach a fuller understanding than if they are perceived separately. Were an underachieving lower-class student to link educational failure to social class, he would more likely impute significant responsibility for his failure to educational institutions than a student who does not see that relationship. Through the establishment of connections it would thus be possible to comprehend and transcend the subjectivity of a personal condition.

In brief, an individual's language operates as an "internal censor" mediating experience and verbal stimuli. If the semantic, vocabulary, and syntactic levels of his language are limited, the individual is not likely to develop his full potential. This restriction would have several consequences since the verbal mediation that language entails "facilitates further learning, which controls behavior and which permits the development of conceptual thinking." [8]

Language and cognition are two factors that cannot be separated. French studies indicate that by the age of eight deaf children's ability to order terms into word families and their general mental development can be retarded by as much as two years.[9] Evidence of the impact of linguistic factors on cognitive development can be found in studies by Joseph B. Casagrande and John B. Carroll and Aleksandr R. Luria and F. Ia. Yudovich. Recent research by E. Olim, R. Hess, and V. Shipman[10] also shows that linguistic exposure furthers the development of abstract thinking.

What is relevant for this argument is the fact that the type of language an individual internalizes influences his cognitive development as well as his perception of himself and his environment. As will be demonstrated in the following chapter, the absence of sufficient conceptual development and of certain value predispositions, which is related to both socialization patterns and language codes, can prevent the individual from understanding the political code of society at large.

LANGUAGE AND POLITICS

Language can be understood as a cultural and political guidance system into which values handed down from the past are deposited. It provides the group or individual the means to identify with a given culture or political entity. Current linguistic conflicts in Canada and Belgium provide examples of minority groups which view their culture as endangered because the use of their language is being subordinated to that of the prevailing one. The reverse can be observed in countries where language becomes a unifying force. The emergence of nationalism in nineteenth century Germany cannot be separated from the codification of the German language. Nationalists, such as Johann G. von Herder and the Grimm brothers, were aware of the fact that the linguistic diversity in Germany was a deterrent to the unification of the fragmented empire.

The same principle underlies the propagation of the Russian language after the revolution in areas which had indigenous languages. Stalin reorganized the educational system in order to establish the dominance of Russian.* [11] After World War I France and Belgium eliminated German from public education in the Alsace and Malmedy areas, respectively, in order to destroy the link it provided with the Weimar Republic. Other examples of the political weight of language could be drawn from language debates in the Third World and linguistic reforms in China.[12]

Language, serving as an integrating or differentiating element, has, therefore, a political function. It must be taken into account in any analysis of political communication. It is an important factor which is determined, not only by the social context of a society, but by political institutions and interests as well. Both socially restricted language and politically manipulated language

---

* It should be noted, however, that Stalin formally allowed for the maintenance of cultural autonomy and indigenous languages provided that Russian was taught as a parallel language.

can function as agents promoting the stability—whatever its attributes—of a political order.

Language and political consciousness are elements that go hand in hand and that determine the way in which the individual relates to his environment. As noted over a century ago by Karl Marx and Friedrich Engels,

Language is as old as consciousness, language is practical consciousness, as it exists for other men, and for that reason is really beginning to exist for me personally as well; for language, like consciousness, only arises from the need, the necessity, of intercourse with other men.[13]

If the linguistic and cognitive capacities of an individual are sufficiently developed, he is able to engage in effective political communication. Effective communication presupposes, however, that the communicative situation is relatively free of "noise" or those factors that distort communication. The term "distorted communication" designates all forms of restricted and prejudiced communication that by their nature inhibit a full discussion of problems, issues, and ideas that have public relevance.

Emphasis is placed on three forms of distorted communication: directed, arrested, and constrained. Directed communication, dealt with in this chapter, results from governmental policy to structure language and communication. Arrested communication, discussed in Chapter 2, refers to the limited capacity of individuals and groups to engage in political communication because of the nature of their linguistic environment (a restricted speech ·code) and not because of any apparent political intervention. Constrained communication, as will be demonstrated in Chapter 3, denotes successful attempts by private and governmental groups to structure and limit public communication in order that their interests prevail. Directed, arrested, and constrained communication interfere with open political communication since the intentional and unintentional distortions they cause preclude the articulation of demands as well as an unobstructed discussion of specific issues. Moreover, those subject to distorted communication may not be able to recognize the form and consequences of this type of communication.

A critique of distorted political communication is facilitated if a model of open, nondistorted communication can be visualized. In such a model the communicative partners, be they individuals, groups, or classes, would share a similar stock of semantic, syntactic, and lexical knowledge. The ability of all participants to analyze and synthesize would be more or less equal, and there would not be too great a difference in cognitive faculties.[14] Nondistorted communication implies that those engaging in communication would not be separated by attitudes which create social distance and that they would be sharing similar or mutually comprehensible expectations and values. In such a model, the boundaries between private and public language would be suspended in the sense that groups or individuals could articulate their deprivations and aspirations in public and no longer have to confine their discussion to the private sphere. Definitions and interpretations of symbols inherited from the past and emerging in the present would be independent of vested interests which bias communication. Furthermore, the rules, embedded in the belief system of the participants, according to which political phenomena are interpreted, would be flexible. New information could therefore be integrated. These flexible rules would allow for communication about the basic assumptions underlying the political system, even if this communication were to entail a reformulation of these assumptions. The channels of communication of society at large—as represented by mass media and educational institutions—would be accessible to all members of the political community, and there would be a structural possibility for competing ideologies to gain significant public expression.

The above model obviously has no historical counterpart. Politically, it is closer to the goals of the liberal ideology than to any reality. It serves, however, the purpose of providing a yardstick against which distorted communication systems can be measured. Such systems differ primarily from the above model by the fact that they preclude the creation of a public which might influence or control the policies of those in power.[15]

Because open communication can threaten the political status quo, public debate may be limited to topics and issues which are not critical.[16] This type of distorted communication can be effected through censorship, directed communication, and constrained communication. We know of censorship throughout history—from the Index of the Catholic Church, the persecution of Rousseau, the impounding of seditious material, even in the United States, during World War I [17]—to current practices in Greece, Spain, Latin America, and most of the socialist countries.* [18] Directed communication is of interest to us since it is an exemplary case of politically distorted communication and vividly demonstrates the crucial function of language in politics. It can be understood as the attempt to influence the use of language and interpretational schemes by means of overt governmental intervention in the mass media and the educational system. Directed communication in Fascist and Socialist Germany will be discussed at length in the next sections.

The question as to whether distorted communication is equivalent to manipulation has been left open thus far. Obvious objections to the use of the concept manipulation are that it is difficult to measure the effects manipulative attempts have and that it is impossible to define with certainty the interests of a person or group who is allegedly manipulated.

Insofar as language is concerned, the argument could be made that once a language is internalized, there would be no possibility of manipulating it since the speaker of the language would preserve the original meaning embedded in its symbols and signs. In modern society, however, the individual is exposed to institutions, such as the mass media and educational systems, which are subject to indirect and direct political influence or control. It is unlikely that he can disconnect himself completely from that

* The nature of censorship has been covered adequately in the literature and will not be discussed here.

part of the world around him and thus avoid possibly distorted communication. Further, in order that one's symbolic structures of meaning be preserved, social reinforcement is necessary.[19] That the meaning of words can be conditioned and that meaning can be transferred even to nonsense syllables has been successfully shown in experimental settings.[20] In other words, there is no reason why an individual should preserve the meaning attached to a symbol or word at any one point in his life.

The more plausible argument against the use of the concept manipulation would be the difficulty of defining the interests of a person or of a group. One could say that a person is deprived only if he feels deprived. If he does not perceive a material or ideal need as falling within his range of interests, he cannot be considered deprived. If we follow this line of reasoning, the concept of manipulation could be used only if a person or a group is persuaded to relinquish publicly expressed demands or aspirations and accept the status quo. Patriotism may thus be offered as a substitute for better wages; or subjectively plausible but false explanations may be given as to why an individual's or a group's underprivileged position cannot be altered. For instance, "cultural deprivation" has been used as an explanation for the inability of public schools to provide a good education for lower-class students and as a justification for preserving the educational status quo.

Other types of deprivation exist objectively but are not necessarily perceived subjectively. A group may be denied voting rights but not experience this as a deprivation since that situation has been acccpted as part of its social or cultural reality. Another example is that members of the lower classes have a life span which is significantly shorter than that of other groups. Limitations on civil rights and life chances are objective factors, even if those concerned do not make an issue out of them. There exists no plausible justification in any theoretically egalitarian society for the enjoyment of certain groups, but not others, of voting and of living longer since neither civil rights nor life chances can be reduced to a function of individual merit. It would seem that the same holds true for the decision-making process. Unequal distribution of political power cannot be reconciled with the ideal of equal representation for all, irrespective of race and social class. The intentional or unintentional suppression from public debate of the above disparities is equivalent to manipulated, thus distorted, communication.

The demand for the elimination of deprivations cannot be ignored if they are determined primarily by the social position of an individual or group. Deprivations which are not related to social position but which are engendered by an advanced capitalist society as a whole also fall into the range of the individual's objective interest regardless of whether he perceives them or not. The latter type are those arising out of conditions such as environmental pollution, the urban crisis, and the growing imbalance between social and industrial infrastructures.

Language codes and socialization patterns can obscure the perception of social needs and societal problems. In short, the recognition of certain needs and their relative importance requires cognitive skills and political awareness. Both tend to be limited for large segments of the population. If this lack of skill and awareness is not offset by secondary socialization agencies, such as educational and informational institutions, individuals and groups cannot recognize what is in their interest and that of the population at large. The element of manipulation comes into play if these secondary socialization agencies reinforce deprivation by propagating rationalizations or by avoiding pertinent discussion.* The functions of

---

* It is obviously not the task of secondary socialization agencies to undermine the political order by concentrating on social problems which cannot be solved at a particular stage of economic development. Neither can educational institutions and the mass media transmit, in toto, values which are contrary to the legitimating belief system on which the political order is built. High school courses in civic education will hardly have as their primary focus principles of Socialism, nor will they propagate the idea that the authority of governmental institutions has a religious foundation. Nevertheless, these secondary socialization institutions contribute to the formation of the citizen and have thus a definite political function. They influence the consciousness of the individual by acquainting him with the political conventions and ideals of his society and by providing interpretations of the conflicts and

educational institutions and the media will therefore be taken into account in the following two chapters which deal with arrested and constrained communication, respectively.

DIRECTED COMMUNICATION

More often than not the political vocabulary of governments is distorted since words chosen to describe conditions and policies are quite different from their meanings. Two recent examples, "pacification program" and "free fire zone," disguise unintentional genocide. While this abuse of language frequently can be observed in politics, it is not identical to directed communication which is an overt, organized effort to manipulate language.

Directed communication usually occurs in political systems where all social and economic institutions are avowedly subordinated to the interests of one group or party. Totalitarian systems consciously manipulate language and ideas through the rigid control of educational institutions and the mass media. The imposition of the ideology of the totalitarian system usually takes the form of a reinterpretation of all prior history and the elimination of references to any interpretative scheme other than the dominant one. Whereas in advanced capitalist societies the public appears to be depoliticized because of affluence and the decision-making process left to political and technical experts, totalitarian societies ideologize the public to an extent that all acts, even those of daily life, have political overtones. As a part of a ubiquitous political totality, the individual "participates" in politics while remaining politically powerless.

In Germany during the Third Reich and in the [East] German Democratic Republic following World War II, attempts were made to adjust the language to the needs and goals of the political

---

problems which society, and ultimately each citizen, faces. An unrestricted discussion of these issues permits, potentially, the development of the awareness of individuals and groups with respect to their own sociopolitical situation and the conditions of society at large.

order. Mass communication was directed from above, and the constant reaffirmation of the status quo served to stabilize these societies.

The Case of National Socialist Germany

Language manipulation in the Third Reich was not supported by any specific theory incorporated into the Nazi ideology. It was a policy that arose out of pragmatic considerations. Its instruments of manipulation were educational institutions and the mass media. In 1933, a short time after the National Socialists took power, high school students had to take special courses covering the ideology of Fascism, the political personalities of the Third Reich, and the "historical mission" of the National Socialist movement. One of the essential objectives was to acquaint the students with the terminology of the government in order to provide "an identical evaluation of events, even as far as the use of language (Sprach Regelung) was concerned." [21] The ideological goal of these courses was the transmission of fixed definitions and interpretations.[22] The mass media was centrally controlled and supervised by the department of propaganda (Reichspropagandaministerium). The Office of the Press (Reichspresseamt) was in charge of periodicals, and the Office of Literature (Reichsschrifttumskammer) supervised the publication of all books and journals. No channels remained open for the expression of independent or opposing views, and control was rigorously enforced by trying for treason those journalists who deviated from the language regulations issued by the Office of the Press.* [23] Virtually all publications conformed to the dominant ideology. Even academic journals were forced to incorporate the terminology of fascism. The language of professional articles in fields as diverse as history and medical science was distorted and pervaded by an anti-intellectual bias and Germanic traditions.[24] The destruction of all professional

---

* The Facist term for this enforced consensus is *gleichgeschaltet* and cannot be translated precisely. This term has its origins in electromagnetics and conveys the image of something being "switched to uniformity."

societies and political associations eliminated a basis for the articulation of alternative demands and opposing interests.

Standard dictionaries and encyclopedias were revised by deleting terms, adding new ones, and redefining others. These alterations constituted a direct intervention in the use of language. A revised encyclopedia, *Meyers Lexicon,* was published in 1936. From this work Christa Berning extracted a list of new and redefined terms. The following three tables present examples from Berning's research which give an idea of the mechanisms of language manipulation.[25]

*New Terms***

Ahnenpass	certificate of ancestry
Arbeitstrasse	a race which by nature engages in hard work
artecht	original, true to its species (race)
Aufartung	"goal of race hygiene" (i.e., improvement of "racial stock")
Aufnordung	"to enlarge the area of the Nordic race"
Blitzkrieg	rapid war of movement
Blutbewusstsein	consciousness of one's blood
fremdvölkisch	coming from a different population
Geburtenkrieg	war based on births (a term denoting the competition among countries with respect to increases in population)
germanische Demokratie	Germanic Democracy
Kulturdünger	"Term denoting those populations (Völker) which possess a high racial and cultural standing, but which mix with less developed ones. They fertilize the culture of the less developed populations but decay in that process."
Rassenbrei	melange of races
Rassenschande	marriage to or intimate relationship with a non-Aryan, equivalent to "blemishing one's race."

** The definitions in quotation marks are those from the *Meyers Lexicon.* The meaning of the other terms is reconstructed by the author.

Reichsbräuteschule	imperial school for brides
Veradelung	process leading to the establishment of an elite
Verstädterung	urbanization (with a negative connotation)
Volksempfinden	the people's sentiment
Volksschädling	a person who harms the people's interest

In addition to the incorporation of new terms, redefinitions of standard terms indicate the regulated nature of the language. The following table lists (1) definitions of terms which were used in the edition of *Meyers Lexicon* published under the Weimar Republic in 1924 and (2) the reformulation of these terms as they appeared in the revised *Meyers Lexicon* of 1936.

Prefascist and Fascist Definitions

I—definition of term during the Weimar Republic
II—definition of term during the Third Reich

Abstammungsnachweis	I "see under 'cattle breeding' "
	II "genealogical certificate of Aryan origin"
Arbeitsdienst	I "see under 'constraint to work' "
	II "great educational institution for the National Socialist people's community"
Blutschande	I "incest"
	II "intimate relation with a non-Aryan"
Blutvergiftung	I "toxemia; blood poisoning"
	II "appearance of decay in people and races"
fanatisch	I fanatic; adjective that has negative connotations
	II fanatic; adjective that has positive connotations
hart	I hard; adjective that has negative connotations
	II hard; adjective that has positive connotations
Intellect	I "creative capacity"
	II "as distinguished from instinct . . . a term denoting a critical, subversive, and destructive quality"

Konzentrationslager	i	"... camps established by Great Britain for the Boers . . . where women and children perished in masses"
	ii	"Better term to be used is 'Detention and Education Camps.' . . . They have the purpose of educating the enemies of the National Socialist State . . . of making them harmless and transforming them into useful members of the community (Volksgenossen)."
organisch	i	organic
	ii	"a positive attribute . . . denoting what has been grown from blood and soil, e.g., organic philosophy which eludes the tyranny of the schemes of reason."
rücksichtslos	i	inconsiderate
	ii	". . . a term that has a positive meaning denoting resoluteness and energy. Describing the enemy, it preserves its old connotations."
Hass	i	hate
	ii	hate has a positive meaning if applied to the right side. "The heroic hate of the Nordic race is strongly contradictory to the cowardly hate of the Jewry."
Züchtung	i	breeding
	ii	breeding. "There really has been a rebirth of the nation because of the conscious breeding of a new man."

It is interesting to note that those who reformulated the language not only created new terms but redefined words to signify just the opposite of what they meant before the advent of Fascism.

The rational basis of language was subverted by the overuse of (a) mechanical and organic terms such as *kraftströmend* (to be full of flowing power), *stählern* (to be like steel), *sich aufgeladen fühlen* (to feel charged with power), and *Ausrottung* (elimination); (b) terms evoking a mystical attitude toward politics like

Volksgemeinschaft (community of the people); and (c) totalizing superlatives such as *abgrundlos* (without perceivable limits) and *unvorstellbar* (unimaginable).

Words normally used to describe inanimate objects were applied to man and society. Thus the ideal German was like steel (*stählern*) and lived in an organic community of people (*organische Volksgemeinschaft*) which was charged with power (*aufgeladen*) as a result of predestination (*Vorsehung*). Man became depersonalized. Being *gleichgeschaltet* (switched to uniformity), the individual was part of a process that was directed from an unperceivable source called Volksgeist (the spirit of the people). Organizations and objects were described with adjectives normally reserved for people or other living beings.

Terms and phrases like the "flow of history" (*Geschichtsfluss*) and the "spirit of the people" (*Volksgeist*) pre-empted the importance of individual action. Words and symbols gained a power of their own and ceased to represent anything rational. The rhetoric of the public subsumed the private. Victor Klemperer, a German philologist who lived during the Third Reich observed, "the language of the Third Reich does not know a private realm as distinguished from the public one. Everything is speech and everything is public. 'You are nothing, your people are everything' [*Du bist nichts, dein Volk ist alles*]. This means you are never alone with yourself or with those of your kind, you are always in front of your people." [26]

The intellect was regarded as negative, and irrational drives were described as sane. Göring thus commented on the attempt on Hitler's life in 1944: "The powers of the instinct are overcome by the powers of such diabolic intellect." [27] Meaningful communication between individuals was impossible since large scale regimentation eroded trust. In this cognitive isolation the ability to remain rational was assaulted. "If a lie comes from all sides to me, if the number of those persons on my side who doubt it becomes smaller each day with no one left at the end, then I will be overpowered by it at some time too. . . . Propaganda which has been recognized as lies and boasts, will be successful if one is energetic enough to perpetuate it." [28]

A content analysis of political and popular publications of the period reveals a new and repetitive use of terms and words which were not officially redefined. Most of the terms, especially adjectives and nouns derived from verbs, were part of specialized vocabularies such as those of the physician, the biologist, the soldier, and the technician. Public communication was characterized by a relentless repetition of slogans, emotive terms, and superlatives. The flexibility of language was impaired by a freezing of the contents of symbols and an excessive use of nouns and the passive mode.

Another instrument of language manipulation was orders issued by the Office of the Press stipulating terms to be either utilized or abandoned in newspaper reporting. Originally called Language Regulations, the name of the orders was later changed to Daily Directives from the Secretary of the Press. Below are a number of these directives listed in chronological order. [29]

Date	Directive
June 24, 1933	"The term 'German-Austrian Incorporation' can no longer be used."
March 20, 1934	"It is requested that the term 'People's Day of Mourning' be replaced by the term 'Memorial Day for the Heroes'."
April 14, 1934	"For obvious reasons, the Nationalist Socialist concept of blood and soil cannot be used in the propaganda designated for colonial areas."
Sept. 1, 1934	"Prime Minister Göring's statement 'The German people must become a people of pilots' has to disappear from the German press since considerations of foreign policy require it."
January 6, 1936	"It should be pointed out that there is a new style, 'the German style,' which is based on the [German] relationship to race. The term 'German style' has to be entered into the public consciousness."

Date	Directive
August 22, 1936	"The 'Führer' has ordered that in the future the term 'victims [*Gefallene*] of the movement' must be replaced by 'the assassinated of the movement.' This will make it clear that the National Socialist fighters did not lose their life to honest enemies, but to hideous murderers."
Sept. 1, 1936	"The following has definitely been decided upon for the names of the different powers in Spain: The 'Franco Government' has to be called the 'Spanish National Government,' the others can never be mentioned in connection with the term 'government.' Their name is simply 'Bolsheviks.' "
January 14, 1937	"The concept 'race' cannot be used for advertising. It is not permissible to use the term to promote a new hat style or an automobile engine."
July 27, 1937	"According to the new government, the term 'propaganda' is a legally protected one, so to speak, and cannot be used in a derogatory sense. . . . In short, 'propaganda' only if it serves us; 'agitation' for those who are against us."
December 13, 1937	"The urgent directive has been given that the term 'League of Nations' can no longer be used by the German press as of today. This word no longer exists."
March 21, 1938	"This is a strictly confidential clarification of the directive which stipulated that the term 'Great Germany' cannot be used in reference to the annexation of Austria. . . . We have to avoid the impression that the German demands are fulfilled because of the German-Austrian unity. This is not the case. Obviously, there are many other areas which belong to the real Great German Empire and which we will claim in due time."
January 14, 1939	"This is a strict directive to the German press: In future times Adolf Hitler can only be called 'Führer' and not 'Führer and Chancellor.' "

Date	Directive
September 1, 1939	"The word 'war' has to be avoided in all news coverage and editorials. Germany is repulsing a Polish attack."
September 11, 1939	"The word courageous can only be used for German soldiers."
November 16, 1939	"The term 'peace' has to be deleted from the German press."
June 9, 1941	"Be reminded once again that the U.S.A. Jew, [sic] Baruch, cannot be attacked. He is a 'protected Jew.'"
August 14, 1941	"The army demands that the term 'fighter planes' be reserved for German planes only."
October 16, 1941	"There should be no more references to Soviet or Soviet Russian soldiers. At most they can be called Soviet army members [*Sovietarmisten*] or just simply Bolsheviks, beasts, and animals."
June 3, 1942	"The term 'patriotic' can no longer be used, even in its positive sense."
March 16, 1944	"The Secretary of Propaganda and People's Enlightenment has requested that the term 'catastrophe' be completely deleted from the German language. It has therefore been decided that the word 'catastrophe' be replaced by the term 'large emergency' and 'catastrophe aid' by 'air war aid.'"

The Language Regulations dealt with almost every phase of public and private life, the banal as well as the substantial. They reflected the idiosyncrasies of the leaders and indicated future action. But the regulations also helped to obfuscate indications foreboding the breakdown of a political system. A linguistic plausibility structure was imposed from above which validated actions and policies by rendering them believable. In the Third Reich, the messages communicated were unequivocal and unqualified. No subtle variation in interpretation was possible. Labels were provided for friends and enemies to facilitate identification. If the Russian soldier were typified as a beast and not as a human being and if this label were accepted by most of the population, then there would be no reason for not taking his life when he was captured.

The acquired language became part of the common sense structure and was validated through the attitudes and actions it induced. Research indicates that if a stereotype or a label is successfully attached to a group, the attitudes of those confronted with members of that group will be influenced accordingly.[30] It has been acknowledged by Vietnam veterans that the atrocities committed by them against the civilian population were facilitated psychologically by the designation of the Vietnamese as "gooks" or "dinks," that is, subhuman species.[31] Labels make the killing more acceptable. In addition, the labels can be justified a posteriori by the very act they precipitated. Thus, quite a number of people in Germany felt after World War II that something must have been wrong with the Jews since so many of them were put into concentration camps.

The obvious question arises as to whether this language of the Third Reich, which evoked emotions, humanized objects, and mechanized man, was accepted by those who were exposed to it for twelve years. Since it has proven impossible to measure ex post facto the efficiency of the distortion of language during the National Socialist era, this question will remain empirically unanswerable.[32] However, it seems that in a situation like that which Hannah Arendt calls "total domination," the individual can speak only the language of those who dominate him. The language in Fascist Germany was such that it could not be tested against reality. The very diffuseness of its symbols, its mystical, technical, and archaic character eluded rational examination. Klemperer described how people who were opposed to Fascism unknowingly employed its terms and how others kept using them even though the society for which they were created was collapsing.[33] Another indication of the effectiveness of the manipulation of the public resides in the fact that until the very end of the war there was no visible opposition to the system other than that by small groups. The "total state"—a term propagated as early as July 1933[34]—

of the National Socialist system was successful in imposing distorted communication since, as a contemporary communications expert stated, "all channels are under the complete control of the propagandist and no counter-arguments are ever presented in any media." [35]

The point is that the linguistic regulations of the Third Reich contributed to the integration of individuals and groups into that society.[36] And one can say that the manipulation of language helped to delay the collapse of the political system.

The Case of East Germany

After World War II, distorted communication occurred in East Germany similar to that in National Socialist Germany. Apart from the need to eliminate terms and definitions which originated in the Fascist period, expressions relating to politics and economics had to be adapted to the socialist ideology.[37] Even though the subsequent comparison of the East German language to the West German one indicates that the language of postwar Socialist Germany was distorted to a lesser degree than that of the Third Reich, the regulation of political communication was and is such that it can be subsumed under directed communication.

The regulation of political communication was better organized in East Germany than in the Third Reich, although there were no attempts to eliminate specific terms by administrative order. In addition, socialism, unlike national socialism, provided a more rational and thus more persuasive ideological framework. Modifications in language were brought about as a result of government control of the mass media, publications, and educational institutions; all organizations and associations were incorporated into socialist ones and deprived of any meaningful political function.

The language was administered through a sophisticated control system headed by the Section for Agitation and Propaganda of the Central Committee of the Socialist Party. Unlike the National Socialist Office of the Press, this department had a strategy for its propaganda program. Selections were made of topics to be elaborated, arguments to be advanced, news items to be covered, and even of those persons to be employed as journalists. A journalist who did not conform to official directives was subject to dismissal or prosecution. He had to avoid, as H. Hecht observed in his analysis of the East German press, "comments on events before official versions have been issued, a mediocre treatment of a [political] campaign, the neglect of obligatory arguments . . . the neglect of the order to politicize each article, and the 'crime' of typographical errors which had a distorting effect." [38]

The theoretical justification for the reform of the language was drawn from the Marxist classics. Lenin argued that at the outset of revolutionary change, "our most important task is the selection of language, an artificial, conscious selection that takes place during the current, fundamental process." [39] Stalin referred to "the language revolution . . . which has to be carried out from above," [40] and to language as "a weapon of transformation and struggle." [41] A similar position was taken by some Marxist scholars. The Russian linguist L. O. Reznikow stated, "Marxism teaches us that language reasserts itself not only as a means of communication . . . but also as a powerful tool which can be used to affect thoughts, feelings, and especially behavior, as well as, ultimately, the material reality." [42]

The functions and goals of the regulation of language were aptly described in a standard text book used in the early sixties in Eastern Germany:

The level of achievement in language and the general linguistic culture of our population do not at this time correspond to the level of our social development. There is an urgent need to remedy the situation. . . . We confront the necessity . . . of taking care of the material receptacle of our thought and of making sure that all of our people know how to master this "tool of struggle and of the development of society" (Stalin). . . . The purely linguistic instruction is still hindered by the chains of a formal abstract grammar. The point of departure for all studies should be the content of language. . . .

This [situation] has been caused by neglect of the word as a basis for meaning.[43]

Starting from this premise, changes in language in East Germany, like those of Nazi Germany, consisted of the reformulation of definitions, the deletion of words, the addition of loanwords (especially from the Russian), and the creation of new terms.

Because an edition of the *Duden*, the standard German language dictionary, was published in 1947 and accepted by both Germanys prior to the publication of separate East and West editions, a basis of comparison is available for the analysis of changes in the East German language. In the first East German edition of the *Duden*, published in 1951, all the terms that remained in the 1947 edition which related to the social and economic institutions of the Third Reich and to private property were deleted. (The West German edition of 1961 likewise lacks those terms which are unique to the East German socioeconomic system.)[44] After 1951, East German editions included all new terms incorporated into the West German language.*

Hugo Moser has estimated that the number of newly coined terms in the East German editions was ten times larger than that of the West German editions.[46] Most of the new words coined in East Germany were derived from terms such as peace, youth, and Socialism. Werner Betz compared the 1954 and 1961 West German editions and the three East German editions with the 1947 *Duden*. His analysis of all entries under the letter "A" indicates that there had been changes in the definitions of 200 of the 4000 entries in the East German editions. Among those changes, 25 were politically motivated. Under the same letter of the Eastern Dudens, there were 182 new entries while the West German editions included 22 new entries.[47] Ten of the 182 new

---

* A number of terms originating in the language manipulation of the Third Reich remained in the West German edition of 1961 such as: *Volksdeutsche* (people belonging to the German *Volk*), *Volksgeist* (the spirit of the people), *Nationalgefühl* (national sentiment), *Gemeinschaftsgeist* (spirit of community), and *Volksverrat* (betrayal of one's people).[45]

East German entries had political connotations, such as *Aktiviste-nehrung* (honorary reception for people excelling in political activities), *Arbeiterstudent* (student from the working class), and *auspowern* (to overpower).[48] Close to 10 per cent of all entries under the letter "A" were either new or redefined. The above change in the East German *Duden* may appear minute, but the significance of this linguistic change becomes obvious if one keeps in mind the stability of language. Using a standard list of 100 words, J. H. Greenberg has estimated that there is an average change in Western languages of only 13 per cent over a period of 1000 years. The literature reveals that changes in the vocabulary of a language proceed very slowly and that sudden modifications in the semantic structure of a language do not take place, at least, as our evidence indicates, not prior to the twentieth century.[49]

The editors of the first East German edition of the *Duden* explicitly state the purpose of the lexical revision: "The total vocabulary had to be examined in order to clarify to what extent it corresponds to our use of the language, to our scientific knowledge, and to our views of society. Obsolete and superfluous terms have been deleted. Definitions (*Sinndeutungen*) have been thoroughly reexamined . . . and, if necessary, created." [50]

A comparison of some key terms in the West German *Duden* of 1961 with the East German edition of 1951 indicates ideological differences.[51]

Term	East German definition	West German definition
Atheismus (atheism)	"denial of the existence of God"	"disavowal of the existence of God"
Dialektik (dialectics)	"originally, 'the attainment of truth by argument and counter-argument,' today, 'search for the contradictions in the nature of things . . . for the development of the struggle of opposites' (Lenin)"	"search for the truth by finding and surpassing contradictions, also sophistry"

Term	East German definition	West German definition
Revolution (revolution)	"upheaval of the state, overthrow, abrupt change of a social system, especially of its economic foundation"	"violent upheaval of the state, overthrow"
sozial (social)	"concerning the society, the community; societal, to fulfill one's duties to society"	"concerning the society, the community; societal"

Betz and Moser, in separate studies, compared the East German *Duden* published in 1957 with the West German *Duden* of 1961. The ideological differentiation of the definitions becomes more explicit. The following examples are adapted from their research.[52]

Term	East German definition	West German definition
aufrüsten (to rearm)	"to increase the power of the armed forces for aggressive purposes; also to erect scaffoldings"	no entry
Bourgeoisie (bourgeoisie)	"the dominant class in capitalist societies"	"(affluent) middle class citizens (also people degenerated by a life of luxury)"
Determinismus (determinism)	"doctrine stipulating the objective regularities and causal determination of all phenomena pertaining to nature and society"	"doctrine stipulating the nonexistence of free will"
Faschismus (fascism)	"chauvinistic and frequently terroristic form of imperialism"	"anti-democratic and nationalistic philosophy of the state"
Kapitalismus (capitalism)	"an economic and social order which is based on the private ownership of the means of production and on the exploitation of wage labor"	"an individualistic and social order in which the desire for individual profit is the principal motivation"

Term	East German definition	West German definition
Militarismus (militarism)	"subordination in imperialist states of all societal and governmental areas under military command and concommittant repression of the mass of the population and aggressive foreign policy"	"dominance of military convictions"
Opportunismus (opportunism)	"absence of moral principles; the retreat from difficulties; adjustment to changing (political) situations; . . . the subordination of the class interests of the proletariat to the interests of the bourgeoisie"	"adjustment to changing situations; behavior springing from pragmatism"
Pazifismus (pacifism)	"rejection of all wars, even of the just ones"	"rejection of war for religious or ethical reasons"
Verelendung (pauperization)	"constant process of deterioration in the conditions of workers under capitalism"	no entry
Volksdemokratie (people's democracy)	"state where the toiling masses rule under the leadership of the working class; an organization of the state which corresponds to this situation"	no entry

Both Betz's and Moser's research reveals, as demonstrated below, that the definitions of important political terms were refined, becoming more differentiated ideologically in the three successive East German editions published in 1951, 1954, and 1957.

Term	Edition of Duden	Definition
agitieren (to agitate)	1951	"to recruit"
	1954	"to enlighten, to recruit"
	1957	"to enlighten, to recruit for a party, for a progressive movement, to recruit [a person] in an enlightening way, to [accept] a [political] conviction"
Parlamentarismus (parliamentary form of government)	1951	"restrictions of democratic actions to the activities of a parliament"
	1954	"restrictions of democratic actions to the activities of a parliament"
	1957	"bourgeois form of government in which the parliament formally determines policy"

Today an efficiently organized control apparatus assures that a socialist version of the German language is administered to the population through the mass media and educational institutions. Though the language lacks the mystifying and totalizing symbols of the fascist language, it is more conspicuously influenced by terminology from the sciences, the military, and the state ideology. Since the semantic space is abundantly structured by predefinitions, the individual is hindered in evolving his own interpretations. Language becomes a guidance system with rigid symbols. As S. Pritzwald observed, "Language regulations, which determine the ideological meaning of words . . . result in a state where the written and verbal communication of man follows prescribed lines of the mind. . . . Man can follow a *limited* system of signs and symbols and free himself of individual considerations." [53]

Living in such a society, the individual internalizes a language programmed by political strictures. It is an artificial language resulting from the interest of system maintenance and leads to the reformulation of all terms touching political and economic dimensions of society. Political stereotypes and slogans, reminiscent of George Orwell's "newspeak," structure political perceptions. Wofgang Schöfer's comment on the use of language in the modern state can be well applied to East Germany. "In our times the influence [of language] consists of the typification of the spiritual content. Linguistic clichés, which often have a minimum of content only, constitute communication to a large extent." [54]

In East Germany the language is still German, and, as Betz wrote, ". . . seen from the outside, [it] seems to be preserved, but at the same time it is reformulated in its sema-siological functions [i.e., the transmission of meaning structures]. Attempts are made to move the sema-siological system in a specific direction." [55]

Today the East German language is differentiated from the West German one by the reformulated semantic substructure of the language, by the heavy use of typifications and negativisms, and by a tendency to use a formalized style. In both Germanys, the impact of scientific and bureaucratic codes has led to a decline of the verb and an increased use of nouns. [56]

There is evidence that the administered language has been accepted by the population in East Germany. Both the written and publicly spoken language indicate that the goal of extending the language code of party functionaries to the general population has been attained to a significant degree. An observer traveling in East Germany noted "a definite audible distinctiveness" particularly among younger people. "They spoke something close to the German of the party workers . . . although none of them had ever been a member of the party." [57]

The older generation, however, adjusts only slowly to the new language. [58] H. J. Scherbaum refers to a study on refugees which demonstrates a rift in the use of the German language. In this study conducted in the late fifties, the communist meaning of words was spontaneously provided by 60 per cent of those refugees with a professional background who had terminated their education after 1950, by 40 per cent of those trained between 1946 and

1950, and by 20 per cent of those who completed their education before 1939. The "partial alienation of the vocabulary did not leave untouched the power of imagination." [59]

If an individual has spent most of his lifetime in a political system dominated by directed communication, his language and consciousness will be shaped accordingly. Those who grew up in East Germany were most likely to accept the language of the dominant ideology, but even those who had experienced a different political system could not separate themselves from the distorted language. Thus refugees of all ages who came from East Germany in the fifties needed a number of weeks before they became adjusted to the language of West Germany even though they had opposed the communist system.[60] The manipulation of language was more powerful than their convictions.

2

SOCIAL CLASS AS
THE DETERMINANT OF
POLITICAL COMMUNICATION

"The impact of factual reality," Hannah Arendt argues, "like all other human experiences, needs speech if it is to survive the moment of experience, needs talk and communication with others to remain sure of itself." [1] Any distortion of public or private communication contracts the parameter of politics since a political system depends on communication and since political interests have to be articulated before they can be acted upon or expressed in policy.

Participation of any group in political communication presupposes that it is able to express its rights, claims, or interests, be they material or ideal. Groups holding political power may distort or control this expression of interests, as was seen in the previous chapter, through the manipulation of language and ideas. However, the communication of interests may also be distorted if the group or class concerned is not capable of articulating experienced deprivations and cannot generate from its own base symbols and ideas alternative to dominant ones.

Historically seen, demands of the lower classes were formulated within ideological frameworks provided by intellectuals originating predominantly from other classes. In the nineteenth and early twentieth century, as today, lower-class groups left on their own rarely articulated their political interests although they were subject to deprivations. Not being able to link their deprivation to the structures of society, they and their discontent were bound to remain impotent until catalyzed by outside influences.

No research known to the author demonstrates that the linguistic code and the dominant modes of socialization of a group may influence either that group's participation in the political process or its ability to recognize that its problems are political ones. Murray Edelman has pointed out that political alternatives can be perceived only if language is used in an analytic and synthetic way.[2] However, this instrumental use of language in politics may a priori be impeded by the linguistic code a group shares.

Among the few models connecting language and the social structure, Basil Bernstein's analysis is the most fruitful for the purposes of this study. Following empirical studies, he distinguishes between an "elaborated" language code and a "restricted" code. These two codes are linked, as will be demonstrated, to socialization strategies which, in turn, influence the way an individual relates to society. Both language codes and socialization strategies have a bearing on the type of communication in which the individual engages. What will emerge below is the dialectical relation between the restricted code and arrested communication. The restricted code emanates from a linguistically deprived environment; once acquired the code limits and thus arrests the development of the speaker's innate linguistic and communicative potential.

From this perspective, language and patterns of socialization are potent factors in the political socialization process. This chapter will, therefore, be devoted to an examination of a variety of studies pertaining to the relation between social classes and both language codes and socialization strategies. If significant class-specific variations prevail in linguistic and socialization patterns and if these variations are not overcome by educational institutions (which will be analyzed in the final section of this chapter), predictive statements about the political values and behavior of lower- and middle-class groups and individuals can be made. This permits us to deal with the question as to which groups are likely to adjust to and support the political system and which groups will question the legitimacy of policies and rationales provided from above.

THE SOCIAL STRATIFICATION OF LANGUAGE

Since social classes consist of strata situated along a continuum from the lowest to the highest socioeconomic level rather than of homogenous groups clearly demarcated one from another, significant differences among these classes become apparent only if noncontiguous groups are analyzed. The data used in this analysis are drawn, therefore, from studies of the linguistic patterns of groups coming from the middle and lower classes without considering at length intermediary groups such as skilled workers and lower-level white-collar groups. Moreover, the language patterns of these intermediary groups vary from country to country. A more explicit cultural differentiation among social strata in France and Great Britain does permit the assumption of the likelihood of different language patterns for skilled workers and white-collar employees. Such an assumption is not permissible for the United States and Germany where both these groups more obviously partake of traits of those above and below their stratum.

In this study the term "middle classes" refers to the middle and upper segments of the middle class. Groups in that class consist of persons who have at least some college education, pursue nonmanual occupations, and/or hold professional, technical, or managerial jobs. The term "lower classes" refers to large segments of the working class and the lowest socioeconomic strata. The lower-class group consists of wage earners holding unskilled or semiskilled jobs in the service or production sectors, the unemployed, and the poor; they are persons who have, at the most, some high school education.

The criteria for class position applied by most authors cited here are socioeconomic, that is, social status as defined by education, occupation, and/or income. Furthermore, the qualification that only tentative statements can be made about the linguistic patterns of the uppermost segment of the working class and the lower segment of the middle class also holds true for the discussion of socialization strategies. Data analyzed here are drawn from research conducted in Western Europe and the United States on children, adolescents, and adults.

Because the adult has already internalized the language specific to his group, it is extremely difficult for him to switch to the language pattern of another group. Most people will use the speech code of the group into which they are born all their lives, unless they succeed—after overcoming tremendous cultural and educational obstacles—in joining another group or class. (One must keep in mind that most social mobility in advanced industrial societies is within social classes rather than between social classes.) It seems therefore justifiable to extrapolate adult linguistic and cognitive behavior from research on children and adolescents.

Class-specific differences in the acquisition and handling of language have been found among children as young as twelve months. In a study of six-month to four-year-old French children, Odette Brunet used a comprehensive development coefficient which included articulation capacities.[3] At the age of six months, working-class children had a slight advantage of two points over their middle-class peers, but this relation was reversed at the age of one year when retardation of language development among working-class children set in. Brunet's test of children's cognitive capacities, as measured in the construction of objects, revealed that in each group the percentage of children succeeding in the task increased with age; however, the number of middle-class children who succeeded was by far larger than the number of working class children who did so. By the age of four there was a differentiation of nineteen points in favor of middle-class children. Brunet cites a study by Kohs and Goldstein in which an identical test was used except for the addition of a visual aid. That study showed a success rate of 18 per cent among middle-class children and 11 per cent among working-class children. Working-class children growing up in institutions evidenced the most severe delay in their intellectual development.

British tests also showed significant variations in the use of grammar and vocabulary between middle- and working-class children. The form of speech and speech content were different in both groups, the middle-class group exhibiting earlier speech maturation.[4] This phenomenon can be shown to exist elsewhere. Replicating Bernstein's model (which will be discussed at length), Peter M. Roeder observed class-specific modes of articulation among West German children. Sentence structure of German working-class children was less complex than that of middle-class children, and more grammatical mistakes, particularly in the use of nouns and verbs, were made. Children from a higher socioeconomic status used more qualifying clauses in their sentences and applied adjectives of a more abstract nature.[5]

A study of the relation between speech maturation and parental occupational status among American children demonstrated that the higher the socioeconomic position of the parents, the more likely it was for language development to have taken place at an early age. Conversely, children of parents working in the lowest paid occupations were more likely to have articulation defects.[6] Similar phenomena were observed by Vera P. John, who reported that American "children from high income status families have been found to speak in longer sentences, more articulately, and with a more varied vocabularly than do their lower class peers."[7] The lower-class child has difficulty identifying action words and words which are uncommon to his or her environment. His ability to classify objects is not as well developed as that of the middle-class child, in part, because the lower-class child tends to concentrate on attributes which are not essential to the identified object.[8]

In the largest research project on language behavior carried out so far in the United States, Martin Deutsch tested more than

100 factors related to the linguistic and cognitive behavior of nearly 2800 children from various ethnic groups and social classes. One of the significant results of his work concerns the relative weight of class position and race as variables having a bearing on language development. Deutsch's study leaves no doubt as to "the evidence that the cognitive repertoire of Negro and white children can be similar as well as different, as it tends to be on I.Q. and certain other tests. Further, when the number of significant correlations of language with SES [socioeconomic status] level are considered, it becomes clear that socio-economic status is a more powerful determinant of language behavior than is racial membership." [9] On specific tests, such as the vocabulary measure, "class membership retains its cumulative effect . . . despite the control on race, i.e. even within the Negro and the white groups." [10] This finding is supported by evidence from other studies on the impact of socioeconomic status on language and cognitive learning in black groups.[11] Ellis G. Olim demonstrated that the elaborated code of black middle-class mothers was related positively to superior cognitive performance of their children, and the restricted code, characteristic of lower-class subjects, to inferior performance.[12]

The 2800 children in Deutsch's "verbal survey" were first and fifth graders. Among the fifth graders, out of 52 selected variables related to cognitive functions and language ability, 22 correlated significantly with socioeconomic status. Fifteen of the 52 variables correlated on both the first and fifth grade levels. Ten of these 15 variables proved to have a higher correlation in the fifth than in the first grade. Compared to middle-class children, the lower-class children regressed in areas crucial to language development. Of the ten variables, the first three indicated a relative decline of I.Q., a phenomenon also observed by Kenneth Clark in his study of children in Harlem schools.[13] The remaining seven dealt with vocabulary, verbal fluence, and comprehension of the sentence structure of teachers and peers. As Deutsch noted elsewhere, "lower class children . . . less often replaced the exact missing word [in the teacher's speech sample], less often filled the deletion with a contextually meaningful response, and less often were able to substitute for the deleted word a word correct in grammatical form." [14]

Among the twenty-two variables that correlated positively with socioeconomic status on the fifth grade level were verbal identification (ability to use a correct noun, adjective, or verb to describe a scene), the capacity to use correct classificatory concepts and to explain the reasons for the choices made, the child's general knowledge, and the ability to provide symmetric responses, that is, to respond to a stimulus word with words of the same grammatical form.[15] Comparative retardation of lower-class children was evidenced in the manner in which they formulated descriptions, using "more self-referent pronouns, fewer different verbs, and less complex verb stems," their speech being "organized at a much simpler level." [16] The study indicated that the reverse is true for children from a higher socioeconomic status whose speech is marked by a more diversified vocabulary, smoother flow, less redundancy, and a more complex and rational organization. This pattern appears to be influenced by the greater exposure to abstract ideas in a middle- or upper-middle-class milieu than in a lower-class environment.

Studies of language stratification of older children and students, such as those done in Great Britain, show a progressive class-specific variation of linguistic performance between the ages of 12 and 15, the grammatical factor being a more decisive element in this differentiation than the lexical factor. This relative retardation of language development of lower-class children corroborates the findings of Deutsch.[17]

Dennis Lawton found that at the age of 12, British middle-class children used passive verb forms more often than working-class children and they tended to use egocentric sentences, subordinate constructions, and complex sentence structures more frequently. Working-class children tended to use active verb forms and sociocentric constructions more often. By the age of 15, these differences were more accentuated, and, in addition, significant differences emerged in the use of uncommon clauses, complex verb stems, uncommon adjectives and adverbs, and personal pronouns. This result is highly relevant in view of the fact that in this test the verbal and nonverbal I.Q. of the children in both groups was described as matched.* Whereas between the ages of 12 and 15 working-class children showed an improvement on the lexical level, middle-class children made notable syntactical advances. Lawton concludes that "social class differences in language are already in existence at the age of 12 and [that] they become increasingly important in the following three years." [18]

In Lawton's content evaluation of the written language of middle- and lower-class children who, as in the tests pertaining to speech, had the same average verbal and nonverbal intelligence, it was demonstrated that those coming from the middle classes had an abundantly more complex and more qualified way of writing than children from the lower classes. More uncommon clauses, adjectives, and verbs were used. Given the fact that writing requires more analytic capacities, it is understandable that the differences in writing would be more dramatic than those in the speech samples. If the use of language presupposes the ability to select between different qualifications and temporal modes, children whose language is structurally underdeveloped will be consigned to undiversified modes of expression. Lawton argues the same point in stating that "working class boys tended to write in a much more descriptive, concrete way than middle class boys. . . . They chose not to write with a high degree of abstraction. . . . The content of the essays reinforces the view that the working class world is dominated by concrete things rather than ideas, by events rather than by reflection upon those events." [19]

The limited lexical and syntactic choices inherent in the restricted code make it difficult for the lower-class student to express his intentions in an explicit verbal manner. In an analysis

* Indicators used by Lawton were Raven's Progressive Matrices and the Mill Hill Vocabulary Scale.

of speech samples, Basil Bernstein also established a rarity of differentiation in the speech of British working-class students. The infrequent use of subordinate constructions, uncommon verbs and adjectives, and grammatical elements which permit qualifications made their statements imprecise, poorly developed, and confined to a low level of generalization. Whereas middle-class students introduced statements with "I think," the working-class students chose the diffuse referent "they." Middle-class students found it necessary to make their meaning explicit since they did not assume a priori that what they intended to say was already known, while working-class students believed that the meaning of their statements was already shared by others. Bernstein pointed out that "on a psychological level [language] codes may be distinguished by the extent to which each facilitates or inhibits the orientation to symbolize intent in a verbally explicit form." [20]

Significant relationships were also found between socioeconomic status and average grades in a study of German academic high school students. Comparing students whose parents were of the working class to those whose parents were professionals, Klaus Heinemann noted class-specific achievements in language and related areas. The difference in language performance persisted until graduation, even though the few working-class students were still in school constituted a highly select group.[21] Analyzing the use of language in German high schools, Regina Reichwein compared lower-middle- to upper-middle-class students. It was found that a significantly higher proportion of upper-middle-class students followed a language pattern similar to the elaborated code. In every age group, students using the elaborated code showed results which were two to three times better in formulating abstractions and generalizations than students sharing a restricted code. Like Lawton and Deutsch, Reichwein observed that the differentiation between groups sharing either the restricted or elaborated speech code increased with the age of the students.[22]

Testing the relation between socioeconomic status and language use among adolescents in France, G. Vincent demonstrated that class-specific language use perpetuated itself even in very selective high schools (*lycées*).[23] As opposed to students from the working class (*classes populaires*, i.e., craftsmen; small shop owners; unskilled, semiskilled, and skilled workers), students from the "cultured classes" (*classes cultivées*, i.e., upper-middle and upper class) scored significantly higher on tasks involving literary and poetic vocabulary, literary exercises, connotations of terms apart from their standard meaning, and the knowledge of abstract terms and concepts. Students from the working class scored better in the use of concrete terms.

Most of these linguistic differences persisted at the university level. In research carried out by Pierre Bourdieu, French university students were stratified according to language use. Whereas differences were no longer found between working-class and upper-middle-class students in the use of terms denoting objects that can be distinguished by sense perception (*langue concrète*), significantly better results insofar as the correct use of terms (avoidance of malapropisms), the ability to define and substitute analogous concepts, and mastery of vocabulary specific to the liberal arts were obtained by upper-middle-class students.[24]

In a study of adult language behavior, M. R. Rosenzweig compared French workers and university students. Like Deutsch, Rosenzweig used the ability to provide symmetric responses as an indicator of class-specific language behavior.[25] According to Rosenzweig, the ability to provide symmetric responses correlates with years of education. In his test, laborers scored significantly lower than students whose origins were predominantly upper-middle class. This result is plausible since in France the worker's education is generally limited to elementary school.[26] In describing the language of the French working class, Pierre Guiraud noted the use of "exaggerations, redundant terms, tautologies, repetitions, and illogical derivations." [27] He also found that the workers are incapable of demarcating objects and situations confronting them because they cannot separate them from the context in which they are embedded. Since they use language primarily in an emotive way, they do not "see the object apart from the reactions and sentiments to which it gives rise." Additionally, the need to express personal values impedes an abstract use of the language.[28]

Pierre Bourdieu has noted in the French working class that there is a "refusal to articulate," and he links this to class ethnocentrism.[29] It seems that working-class groups lack the necessary "distance from language" in order to handle it rationally or in an instrumental way. This "distance" is an individual's consciousness of language, his awareness that language is a tool for both emotional expression and analytic description, and it is the belief that language is a means for the articulation of one's individuality.

Anselm Strauss, in his study of the communicative modes of adults belonging to the lower and the middle classes in the United States, observed phenomena similar to those noted by Bourdieu. His findings parallel those reported earlier. For the sake of brevity, the differences which he observed between the two groups are summarized in the following table[30]:

	Lower Class	Middle Class
1 perspective	fixed perspective; rigid description	use of several standpoints and alternative interpretations
2 organization	lack of clear referents; few qualifications; segmented organizational framework; little grasp of context of event if more than one actor involved	frequent qualifications and illustrations; clear narrative even when narrative is complex; unitary framework of organization
3 classification and relation	relative inability to use categories for people and acts since the speaker tends not to think in terms of classes; imprecise use of logical connections	rich conceptual terminology; frequent classification and use of logical categories

	Lower Class	*Middle Class*
4 abstractions	insensitivity to abstract information and questions	sensitivity to generalizations and patterns
5 use of time	discontinuous; emphasis on the particular and ephemeral	continuous; emphasis on process and development

It is apparent from Strauss' report that Bourdieu's concept of distance from language applies to the way in which adult members of the American lower and middle classes describe situations and events. Members of the lower classes provided sociocentric answers and showed little familiarity with the rituals of middle-class communication. Their socially restricted universe does not require precise statements and refined observations. Thus there is no experience of a need to "be very self-conscious about communicative techniques." [31] Members of the middle classes were comparatively detached from the content of their descriptions and were "sensitive to communication *per se* and to communication with others who may not share [their] viewpoints or frame of reference. . . . People of this stratum can, if required, handle the more complex and consciously organized discourse." [32] A well-developed language permits the individual to articulate intentions clearly and to engage in more precise communication with others. It provides the basis for analytic statements and abstractions which transcend the particular. A language which is limited in its lexical or syntactic dimensions tends to confine the speaker to emotive and concrete expressions.

An individual's language can be so constricted that communication with members of other groups not subject to an identical linguistic and social environment becomes difficult if not impossible.[33] According to Rosalie Cohen, the language of the "hard-core poor" * is distinguished by a predominantly descriptive rather

* R. Cohen and her collaborators estimate that up to 30 per cent of the permanent urban slum dwellers in ghetto areas constitute a group termed "the hard-core poor."

than an analytic mode of abstraction, by great semantic concreteness, by a personalization of objects and groups, by a lack of subtlety and differentiation, and by a tendency to collapse logically distinct categories (e.g., cause and effect, means and ends) into one dimension. Persons speaking this language respond most readily to external features of their environment rather than to abstract qualities. The individual has a discontinuous feeling of time, believes himself to be important only within his social group, is not interested in those aspects of the environment which have no immediate relevance to him, and is more attracted by the unique rather than by patterns and procedures.[34]

The language of the hard-core poor is a restricted speech code in the extreme and contains several features which were reported in the research by Bernstein, Guiraud, and Strauss. Since it cannot be used in an instrumental, reflective way, the language itself, spoken by a person living in starkly deprived conditions, reinforces his social location. The individual's language, cast in the immediacy of his environment, conditions his perception. The categories of his language allow for a grasp of the here and now, but they do not permit an analysis, hence a trenscendence of his social context. Seen politically, this language reinforces the cohesion of a group which shares a specific code, but it can prevent the group from relating to the society at large and to its political institutions. The individual experiences his deprivation subjectively; cognitively speaking, however, he lacks the reference points necessary to perceive the objective reasons for his condition and to relate it to the structure of the society in which he is living. The individual's language thus becomes his internal plausibility structure. In narrowing his ability to discriminate, to conceptualize, and to analyze, it renders his condition more acceptable to him. He is immune from perceiving alternatives.

Basil Bernstein, who has provided the analytic point of departure for most contemporary research on class-specific modes of speech, ascertained, as noted above, the existence of the re-

stricted and elaborated codes.* After numerous testing of speech
and writing samples, the linguistic form of middle-class subjects
proved to be an elaborated (formal) one since it allows for analytic perception and discrimination and for individuated expression of meaning. That of the lower class proved to be a restricted
(public) one since it, as demonstrated as well by Lawton, encourages descriptive thinking and greatly diminishes abstract reasoning.[35] The restricted code is distinguished by its high degree of
predictability. Apart from the lexical limitations of this code,
there are constraints on the syntactic level which reduce the possible range of verbal alternatives. These constraints, however,
cause little problem for personal communication since commonly
shared interests and the individual's strong identification with the
values and norms of his group, reduce the restricted code speaker's need to state explicitly his intent.** Cues to indicate changes
of meaning are transmitted extra-verbally. The content of verbal
messages is less important than the form they take, and emphasis is placed on the latter.[36] This mode of speech is marked by
grammatical simplicity, a uniform vocabulary, short and often
redundant sentences, a scarcity of adjectives and adverbs, repetitive use of conjunctions, and comparatively little verbal differentiation or symbolism.[37] The capacity to formulate generalizations is
therefore restricted. As already observed in the language of the
hard-core poor, categorical statements express simultaneously
cause and effect. Bernstein points to the strictures which this
mode of speech exert on those who speak it noting that

the short, grammatically simple, syntactically poor sentence . . . does
not facilitate the communication of ideas and relationships which re-

* In his early writings Bernstein classified the dominant speech pattern of
the middle class as a "formal" language and that of the lower class as a
"public" language. He subsequently changed these terms to "elaborated" and
"restricted" codes, respectively.
** It should be noted that the middle-class speaker's speech code can approximate a restricted code in certain situations where, prior to communication,
common understandings can be assumed, e.g., in a peer group he can switch to
the restricted code whereas the reverse is not applicable to the lower-class
speaker.

quire a precise formulation. . . . A public [restricted] language does not permit the use of conjunctions which serve as important logical distributors of meaning and sequence. . . . The frequency of, and dependency upon, the categoric statement in *public* language reinforces the personal at the expense of the logical. . . . Traditional phrases . . . tend to operate at a low causal level of generality in which descriptive, concrete . . . symbols are employed aimed at maximizing the emotive rather than the logical impact. . . .[38]

Bernstein specified the qualities of the elaborated code in comparison to those of the restricted one and enumerated several features such as an accurate use of grammar and syntax; complexity of sentence structure and of attendant qualifying conjunctions, relative clauses, and prepositions; a careful use of adjectives and adverbs; and the verbal mediation of individuated meaning.[39] Since the elaborated speaker's code does not limit his use of the syntactic and lexical dimensions of the language, his language performance is relatively unpredictable—in any case less predictable than that of the restricted code speaker. Those who share this code have to convey meaning explictly through language. This in turn implies that language takes on an instrumental character and that the speaker engages in verbal planning. Complex conceptual hierarchies make accurate syntactical and lexical usage possible. Messages exchanged are qualified, and the established causal links are logical. Speakers do not engage in the sociocentric speech observable in the lower classes, but try to depersonalize their speech.

Comparing children who speak the elaborated code to those who speak the restricted code, Bernstein notes that children from the middle classes "learn to scan a particular syntax, to receive and transmit a particular pattern of meaning, to develop a particular [verbal] planning process, and very early learn to orient toward the verbal channel," whereas those from the lower classes "limited to a restricted code will tend to develop through the regulation inherent in the code." Generalizations and concrete, descriptive statements can be transmitted in the latter code, but they involve a "relatively low order of conceptualization." [40]

Almost from birth, the individual acquires the language code specific to his group which in turn provides the matrix for all that he can explore in speech and thought. If the available lexical and syntactic resources are underdeveloped and if arrested communication persists, an individual or group will not be able to select freely among existing perceptual and cognitive alternatives. Their ability to generalize and to use an abstract mode of understanding will be limited. In short, they will be unable to exceed cognitively those social relationships from which the code emanates. Language thus becomes an intervening variable.

The restricted code has essentially a practical function. Speakers of this code are not, however, aware of the existence, functions, or limitations of this code and its descriptive and concrete features. Conversely, the middle-class speaker is aware of his code, of its analytic function and of its potential for perceiving distinctions and grasping generalizations. It becomes apparent that linguistic codes are rooted in the class structure. These codes—as separated by lexical, syntactic, and conceptual boundaries—reinforce the social structure by shaping the speaker's personal and social identity.

CLASS-SPECIFIC SOCIALIZATION AND VALUES

Before entering into the discussion of socialization strategies, it should be noted that no significant empirical research has been done on the possible relation between language codes and socialization strategies. Statements about causal links between language codes and socialization strategies remain, therefore, hypothetical. Neither factor has been shown empirically to be the result of the other. This qualification is important since it dispels the fallacy that linguistic factors determine the nature of socialization and thus the direction of political behavior. Only in combination with specific socialization strategies do linguistic codes create predispositions for political behavior. Where class-specific language codes and socialization strategies coexist, a discussion of the ensuing

political consequences is posssible. Class-specific codes and strategies have their source in specific environmental conditions as
revealed in factors such as educational status, occupational position, or family structure. The subsequent analysis will touch upon
environmental conditions and emphasize the class-specific nature
of socialization strategies.

It has been demonstrated that most of the factors underlying
the acquisition of a restricted code are a product of socioeconomic
deprivation characteristic of lower-class groups. Analyzing background variables which influence a child's reading capacity, Martin
Whiteman specified six factors which are determined by lower-
class status: poor housing, low parental aspiration regarding children's scholastic achievements, large family, lack of conversation,
the absence of cultural and educational activities in early childhood, and nonattendance of kindergarten.[41] The fourth factor
which Whiteman specifies, the absence of conversation during
dinnertime, is indicative of the stinted verbal feedback in the
lower-class family which, combined with an unstable family environment, is directly related to the linguistic retardation of the
child. In Deutsch's words, "strong evidence can be adduced to
support the assumption that it is the active verbal engagement
of people who surround him [the child] which is the operative
influence in the child's language development." [42] It depends,
however, not only on the amount of verbal feedback available to
the child, but also on the quality of the responses. Jürgen Ruesh
analyzed communication from this perspective and developed
the concept of "tangential response." [43] If parents are unable to
pick up the intent of a child through his articulation or action
and therefore give responses which are secondary or tangential to
this intent, the child will be prevented from refining his linguistic
knowledge. If words are acquired without corrective feedback,
the instrumental use of language will be impaired. Meager feedback and the inability of parents to respond to the child's intention frustrates the child thereby undermining his sense of autonomy and emotional stability. An environment penetrated by noise

ruptures the language acquisition process and critically impedes adequate communication between children and parents.[44]

All of these factors are class-specific, but they do not sufficiently explain the over-all relation between social class and language. To date, Bernstein's interpretation of the relationship between language and the social context remains authoritative.[45] According to his view, the formal, grammatical level of language has a great bearing on verbal output. Between language and speech (verbal output) intervenes the social structure. As he states, "the particular form a social relationship takes acts selectively on what is said . . . and regulates the options which speakers select at both the structural and vocabulary level." [46] Different types of social relationships therefore generate different linguistic codes.

Speakers of the elaborated code are socially more isolated since the role relationships are more discrete and receive less support from shared expectations. Meaning must be articulated because it cannot be assumed that others share the speaker's thoughts and feelings. "From a development perspective, an elaborated code user comes to perceive language as a set of theoretical perspectives available for the transmission of unique experience. The concept of self, unlike the concept of self of a speaker limited to a restricted code, will be verbally differentiated." [47] It follows, therefore, that middle and lower-class groups place an unequal emphasis on language and have different perceptual modes with respect to social relations and objects. These environmentally conditioned forms of social relations are structured by contrasting value systems and role arrangements. Bernstein refers to "different normative systems [which] create different modes of social control" [48] and proposes that it is those systems that tend to foster class-specific language codes. What this suggests, in turn, is the existence of class-specific value systems and socialization strategies.

The way in which the individual relates to his social and political environment depends to a great extent on his capacity to decode it, that is, on his language. Whether or not he acts and how he acts upon the environment also depends, however, on the mode of socialization of his class or group, on the educational strategies of his parents, and on the structure of the family into which he was born.

Language has a crucial function in the socialization process. During primary socialization the child can potentially learn to develop and represent his self through the medium of language. The symbols acquired and articulated self-differentiation and individuation. This self-presentation allows the child to develop autonomy. Granted a terrain of his own, the child will express his nascent autonomy through the use of language. Arrested communication in the family, whether it is due to linguistic codes or to the structure of the family, stifles the full intellectual and emotional development of the self, and, as Ronald D. Laing demonstrates, induces in extreme cases a pathological perception of the self.[49]

Research on the "learning problem" reveals that both inhibited emotional development and arrested communication are causative factors in cognitive retardation. Salvador Minuchin observed that cognitive problems are influenced by "a deficit of communication of information through words and the attendant rules which regulate the communicational flow." [50] He emphasized the double-impact distorted communication and specific modes of parental care and control have on the child. An interaction process that is oriented toward the child seems to be the precondition for both self-differentiation and the acquisition of an elaborated language code.

This assumption was tested on a sample of black children and mothers stratified according to socioeconomic status. Observing the interaction between mothers and children, Robert D. Hess reported that middle-class mothers, who as noted earlier provide a cognitively stimulating environment for the children, related to their children in a person-oriented way, whereas lower-class mothers used a mode of communication that was not tailored to the personality of the child. The latter did not explicitly verbalize the meaning of their responses to the childrens' actions, questions, or statements.[51] The number and quality of verbal and emotive responses correlated with the class position of the speaker.

The manner in which parental control is exercised and the understanding parents have of their role as authority figures clearly differentiates middle- and lower-class socialization strategies. M. Hoffman observed that American middle-class parents did not assert their power openly and that they used moral induction as an educational strategy. Their children were meant to acquire as early as possible internalized standards of conduct rather than depend on their parents for supervision and control. They taught their children to modulate their behavior by encouraging them to be aware of the possible consequences it might have on themselves and on others; conversely lower-class parents controlled their children's behavior by invoking parental authority which constituted the sole guideline for their children's action.[52]

Melvin L. Kohn pointed out that working-class parents more frequently punished their children physically, taking into consideration only the immediate consequences of the child's action and not his or her intention. Stressing values that assure respectability, they were more concerned with the child's action than with the child himself. These parents were more likely to assert their power through status appeal, an appeal to their position as authority figures, and placed themselves in the center of the socialization process viewing communication with their children chiefly as a means of transmitting orders. Middle-class parents, on the other hand, took the child's intent into account and respected the child's own principles.[53]

Similar findings for differential control mechanisms are reported in a study by J. Jones.[54] In contrast to working-class mothers, he also found that middle-class mothers tended to choose verbal rather than physical means of control, had a larger and more varied communication with their children, and induced behavior patterns by accenting the child's own preferences. L. G. Benson differentiated between "democratic authority patterns" and "authoritarian authority patterns" and found them to be positively correlated to social status. Parents of high social status showed flexible, democratic exercise of power, while lower-class parents exhibited authoritarian patterns of control.[55]

An authoritarian approach in the socialization of children entails, ipso facto, a denial of autonomy and the emergence of dependency patterns. H. A. Witkin reported that "field-dependent" and "field-independent" personalities originate in socialization strategies which differ sharply in the use of authority.[56] Mothers of field-dependent children tended to inhibit the child's self-development, were more coercive, and provided fewer opportunities for independent behavior and self-representation, whereas those of field-independent children used a more analytic, child-centered approach in controlling behavior and "interacted with their children in a way that tended to foster the development of differentiation of the child." [57]

Field-independence and field-dependence are related to the capacity to sustain role conflict in early childhood. If the ambivalences and discontinuities of changing roles can be integrated by the child, there will be no necessity to habitually invoke external authority agencies. This implies, however, a distance on the part of the child to prescribe norms.* Conversely, if the child's role qua child is typified by the parents, the child will be able to respond less adequately to the tensions engendered in the maturation process. A child cannot establish a balance between his personal and social identities when the former is disregarded by the parents. Recurrent conflicts are suspended and a pseudomutuality or deceptive harmony established. Field dependence is a consequence of rigid role structures in the family and implies a lack of toleration for any change which might threaten its acquired status.

If rigid socialization techniques prevail, the child will over-internalize the roles presented to him and will be unable to de-

---

* Field-dependent individuals are persons who "are likely to change their stated views on a particular social issue in the direction of the attitude of an authority." [58]

velop role distance since no room is left for individuated role interpretations. An inflexible role system in the family makes the development and representation of the child's self outside parental predefinitions very difficult since the child virtually does not exist as an individual in the status-oriented relations of the family. He or she comes to accept external agencies as the sole type of reference points. Only a crippled sense of autonomy can result from this subordination. The parents, in not recognizing the child as an autonomous entity, render the child tangential to their own position. On the contrary, if flexible socialization strategies are used, the child has the possibility of acquiring role distance and of asserting his self with respect to the authority of his parents. As this assures ego identity, the child becomes capable of handling conflicts between his role and the roles of individuals he encounters inside and outside the family. Using the referents of positional versus person orientation and closed versus open communication, Bernstein observed that in lower-class families "judgement and decision making would be a function of the status of the members rather than the quality of the person." Sensitivity to persons is not verbally elaborated, "thus these children are less likely to cope with problems of role ambiguity and ambivalence." In middle-class families, however, "children would achieve a role within the communication system in terms of their unique, affective and cognitive characteristics." [59]

In general, the restricted language code appears to coexist with rigid role structures and modes of socialization, whereas the elaborated one parallels flexible roles and socialization strategies. Roles in lower-class groups tend to be segregated and are strictly defined and separated according to the individual's status, whereas those in middle-class families tend to be differentiated. A high differentiation of roles permits and encourages a sharing of activities and duties. The responsibilities linked to the roles of parents and children overlap. Parental authority is not clearly delimited, and relative moral independence is accorded to the child.

Status-oriented and person-oriented behavior patterns thus are roughly equivalent to rigid and flexible socialization techniques, respectively. The former tends to encourage outer-direction, and the latter self-direction. Outer-direction implies a conformity to externally prescribed rules; self-direction implies the possibility of individuated action that may be contrary to external authority. Self- and outer-directed socialization strategies were observed by Kohn in his analysis of the relationship between social class and value structures. Focusing on parental values, he demonstrated that various dimensions of self-direction and conformity correlated, respectively, with middle- and working-class status. The higher the socioeconomic status of the parents, the more likely it is that they will emphasize self-direction and self-reliance; the lower their status, the greater the stress on obedience and conformity to external authority.[60]

The existence of these values is substantiated by other studies as well. Taking a sample of American families, James W. Swinehart analyzed class-specific child-rearing objectives. According to his analysis, upper-class mothers were oriented toward the social and emotional needs of their children, those from the middle class stressed morality and character, and those from the lower class restricted their attention for the most part to the child's physical needs.[61] John A. Clausen, commenting on middle-class parents, pointed out that they "place considerable emphasis on curiosity, happiness, consideration, and self control. They wish their child to learn to govern himself." Middle-class parents are likely to place great importance on the child's motives and feelings and consciously foster autonomy, self-control, and self-orientation with the implicit goal of individual responsibility and action. If obedience and submission are the dominant values, the child's autonomy is denied. This denial curtails the child's ability to cope with his environment which results in the assumption that the world cannot be mastered rationally.[62]

Also concurrent with rigidity and flexibility are divergent demands and expectations. Reaffirming that higher-status parents are permissive in regard to certain types of behavior, Donald B. McKinley notes the high expectation they have as far as skills and academic achievement are concerned.[63] Parents from the lower classes, on the other hand, generally place less importance on academic achievement.[64] Contained by their immediate life conditions, they are more concerned with their most pressing needs and short-range gratification. They emphasize work and pay, and they themselves feel rewarded by material, rather than ideal, incentives.[65] Similarities to Kohn's and McKinley's studies occur in F. Musgrove's report. Analyzing educational and other values determined by social class, Musgrove found that British middle-class parents held academic, verbal, and literary accomplishments in high esteem while those from the working class had a greater interest in practical, physical, and vocational subjects.[66]

The results of several other studies on the success motivation of children tend to indirectly corroborate these findings. There seems to be a relation between the type of incentive offered to children of different strata and their willingness to respond in a learning situation. In one study the level of achievement for lower-class children dropped if there was no material reward, whereas the achievement of middle-class children increased if there was an ideal reward.[67]

Both socialization strategies and the relationship which people have to language correspond to their positions in the production process. Members of the working class pursue occupations which have little authority. They are subject to regulations coming from above, and opportunities for independent action and self-assertion are distinctly limited. They are used to following rather than giving orders, and their interaction in the work sphere is determined by subordinate relations and strict regulations. Kohn described the class-specific context from which different socialization strategies emanate:

Middle class occupations deal more with the manipulation of interpersonal relations, ideas and symbols, while working class occupations deal more with the manipulation of things. . . . Getting ahead in middle class occupations is more dependent upon one's own actions, while in working class occupations it is more dependent upon collective action. . . . Middle class occupations require a greater degree of self-direction; working class occupations, in larger measure, require that one follows explicit rules set down by someone in authority. . . . At minimum one can conclude that there is a congruence between occupational requirements and parental values.[68]

Persons belonging to middle-class groups experience more autonomy in their occupations and have a greater control over their work. Their principal tools are their cognitive skills, and the instrumental handling of language is an essential prerequisite for their work. The degree of rigidity or flexibility experienced in the work sphere inspires and accentuates specific values which in turn influence the nature of interaction and role playing in the family as well as the socialization strategies applied by the parents.[69] Both the socioeconomic position of the family and the quality of their symbolic interaction become powerful determinants of the socialization strategy which the parents choose. Whether it is a question of parental control mechanisms and values or of dependency relations in the family, significant differences between middle- and lower-class families prevail, differences which have an obvious bearing on political behavior.

Individuation and reflection are prerequisites for understanding politics. In the process of political socialization, the child learns to comprehend political symbols and institutions, to disregard them, or to identify with them. No matter how diffuse acquired values may be, children have political values which can be shown to exist as early as elementary school. By the age of eight, children develop an attachment to political institutions or a distrustful or even cynical view of political institutions. Richard Dawson and Kenneth Prewitt suggest that "as the child begins to become aware of the political world, he simultaneously forms awareness of other societal groupings and definitions of his self in relation to them.

He learns that he is rich or poor, one of a special elite group or of an oppressed minority. . . . Political friends and enemies are formed long before the child fully understands what interests or policy differences actually divide them, and may persist long after such interests or policies actually make any difference." [70] The general orientation of these values as well as the mode in which they are articulated is obviously influenced by the socialization strategies experienced at home. However, there is a more immediate factor, namely, the political values the parents share and their view of society at large. Implicit in the political attitudes of the parents are underlying expectations regarding the political system which are either overtly or symbolically transmitted to the children.

Middle-class parents have a greater sense of independence from political institutions than lower-class parents and, according to Kohn, believe themselves "to be in control of the forces that affect their lives." Lower-class parents feel an inescapable dependency on society and its institutions, a resistance to innovation, and an "intolerance of any belief threatening the social order." [71] These orientations serve as a framework within which the political values of children develop. Given the high correlation between political attitudes of children and those of their parents, it is not surprising that lower-class children are either apathetic with regard to political symbols and institutions or tend to personalize political events. The apathy results from a feeling of powerlessness, and the tendency to personalize ensues from an inability to understand complex phenomena. The sense of powerlessness of lower-class children is probably related to their parents' lack of authority in political matters. Robert D. Hess noted as the most significant social-class difference between middle- and lower-class children, "the tendency for lower class children to feel less efficacious in dealing with the political system than do children from high status homes. . . . Social class differences were large even at the third and fourth grade, and they increased with age. The differences on the efficacy items are among the most striking class discrepancies in the data of this study." [72]

Feelings of powerlessness and uncertainty mean susceptibility to influence from outside agencies.[73] Patterns of dependency and subordination, as we have seen, are more likely to occur in lower- than in middle-class homes.[74] These patterns can lead to an identification with existing political institutions which acts as a deterrent to critical examination of the political process. Thus as Hess states, "lower class children more frequently accept author- ity figures as correct and rely on their trustworthiness and benign intent. There is more acquiescence to the formal structure and less tendency to question the motivations behind the behavior of the government and government officials." [75] Government is seen as needing no change.[76]

The cognitive state of lower-class children that has been demonstrated above also has a bearing on political attitudes since cognitive simplicity and the concomitant lack of flexibility and subtlety in concepts or categories result in a narrow, stereotyped view of political reality.[77] Discussing children's understanding of politics, Hess noted that "the ability to deal with an abstract rather than personalized system is apparently related to cognitive maturity. . . . Working class children also personalized their view of the government. The social class difference may follow from the tendency of the working class parents to emphasize rules rather than offering rationale which are more impersonal and abstract guidelines for behavior." [78]

Various studies cited in Herbert Hyman's analysis of research on political socialization led to conclusions similar to Kohn's and Hess's. According to one study made in the early fifties, lower- class youth scored significantly higher on items measuring explicit and implicit levels of authoritarianism than youth coming from the middle class. They endorsed more strongly the "domination of the strong over the weak" and "obedience to parents." The differences for explicit authoritarianism were not as strong but followed the same pattern. The results of a study of adult political attitudes were comparable in that the degree of authoritarianism was inversely related to class position.[79]

It follows from the above that socialization strategies and language codes can have a politically integrating or alternating function. When sufficient cognitive and symbolic equipment is acquired during socialization, the individual can assert his autonomy in face of external agencies. If there is enough flexibility in socialization strategies, the child's behavior will be delimited by internalized norms and personal judgment; if socialization techniques are rigid and restrictive, the child will be "more conforming, less aggressive . . . more dependent on adults," and exhibit "submissive behavior [and] a dulling of intellectual striving. . . ."[80]

It appears plausible that the repression of conflict expressed in rigid socialization strategies leads to a view of reality as being static and to an extrusion from the individual's consciousness of the tensions engendered by change. To date, little research has been carried out on the question of how the experience of conflict in the family effects children's political attitudes. However, N. Haan found in a study of students' political behavior that conservative students had a minimally conflictual relation with their parents and were raised in families where the educational ideology stressed clear rules, punishments, and rewards.[81] Politically progressive students had the most conflictual relation with their parents and a permissive socialization experience. They were "encouraged by their parents to be importantly affected by their own life experience in their own time and place. . . ."[82] It follows that these students are more likely to feel self-made since subjectively they can attribute their achievement to their own actions rather than to external agents.

As was noted earlier, interests have to be articulated before they can be acted upon and institutionalized. The expression of interests presupposes that a group or class shares a language with which these interests can be articulated and that this language can be sustained even if it runs counter to official, that is, dominant interpretations. The proposition that language and socialization have a decisive bearing on the political values of a group or an individual becomes more apparent if one distinguishes between official and private languages. An official language is an expression of dominant symbols and predefinitions representing the interests of ruling groups. A private language is the expression of individual needs and, possibly, of subordinated group needs. Political stability would presuppose substantial identity between the private and official language, an identity which, however, with the exception of totalitarian societies, is rarely attained.

Political communication becomes distorted when symbols and interpretational rules which are contrary to official symbols and definitions cannot be used publically without sanctions. If contrary and alternative symbols are repressed from official language, they are then confined to the private one, where for technical reasons, control or manipulation cannot be exercised by those in power since they cannot interfere directly with the primary socialization process. If language is seen as the medium for the perpetuation and generation of symbols and meanings potentially contrary to predefinitions imposed from above, a restricted code would provide only a limited basis for a private language and for resistance to official definitions of reality. Moreover, the values of children coming from families with limited linguistic and self-differentiation faculties are more likely, as has been seen, to be supportive of a political system than the values of children coming from families where communication and individuation are encouraged. These predispositions would most likely express themselves in adult behavior patterns that would inhibit the articulation of conflicts and contradictions, especially if they touch on issues exceeding material needs.

To the extent that the official language, as expressed in mass media, educational institutions, and advertising, infringes upon the primary socialization process, external influence over private language is exerted. For middle-class families, however, the realm of private language appears to be relatively broad since the capacity to manipulate symbols inherent in an elaborated speech code combined with a focus on self-direction allows for a defense system against the influence of extrafamiliar socialization agencies. Possession of an elaborated code equals political as well as cultural capital. It makes it possible for an individual to understand and respond to conflicts, whether experienced in the growth process of youth and adolescence or in encounters with external agencies as an adult. The individual can reflect about his experience in society even if external agencies try to reduce the range of symbols which may be antagonistic to dominant political interests. He is able to formulate his own interpretations.

The situation appears different for individuals from the working class. The restricted speech code shared by them, in conjunction with the stress on conformity, does not allow for a questioning of official legitimating rationales; corrosion of these rationales is thus unlikely. The possibility of neutralizing symbols supporting existing modes of domination or control is absent.

The impact which the factors discussed so far have on the political consciousness of groups and thus on political communication is summarized in the table on the opposite page.

SOCIAL CLASS AND
EDUCATIONAL INSTITUTIONS

The family is commonly regarded as the most important agency of socialization since it provides the matrix within which values and norms develop. As we have seen, neither the function of language nor that of socialization can be understood—at least from a sociological perspective—without reference to the family. But since the family loses more and more of its traditional functions to other institutions, among which schools are the most prominent, an analysis of socialization and politics requires a consideration of the role of educational institutions.

Extensive schooling is one of the prominent features of ad-

VARIABLES GOVERNING POLITICAL COMMUNICATION

I. Social class as a determinant of communication

Class Position	1. Language Codes	2. Type of Communication	3. Mode of Reasoning
Lower class	restricted code	nonreflective; implicit meaning	descriptive; concrete
Middle class	elaborated code	reflective; explicit meaning	analytic; abstract

II. Social class as a determinant of socialization

	4. Family Role Structure	5. Modes of Parental Control	6. Strategies of Socialization
Lower class	role segregation	authoritarian; status oriented	rigid; restrictive
Middle class	role differentiation	democratic; person oriented	participatory; permissive

III. Class-specific language codes and socialization as determinants of political values

	7. General Value Orientation	8. Political Dimension of Socialization	9. Political Predispositions
Lower class	outer-direction	conformity to external authority; field dependence	conservatism; authoritarianism
Middle class	self-direction	autonomy; field independence	liberalism; democratism

IV. Modifying elements for both lower and middle classes

10. Exposure to secondary socialization; relative correspondence of secondary socialization with primary socialization
11. Orientation of group or societal ideologies
12. Collective plausibility structures
13. Efficacy of prevailing legitimation of political rule
14. Strategic position in the political bargaining process

vanced industrial society; the democratization of higher education presumably opens the door to all regardless of social or
racial origin. Educational institutions are an integral part of an
individual's socialization; instruction in vocational and cultural
fields prepare one for adult life. Therefore, the argument that
schools could potentially attenuate the effect of class-specific
language codes and patterns of socialization must be taken into
account. The pragmatic component of the contemporary curriculum is complemented by sociocultural instruction, the political
aspect of which helps mold the future citizen. Whether or not
educational experience has a political impact on children depends
on the duration and quality of the education.

A review of the literature indicates that educational achievement depends on motivational patterns and intellectual ability.
Achievement is also influenced by the compatibility between the
culture educational institution transmit and embody and the cultural background of the student. Because socialization strategies
influence motivational patterns and a student's language code has
a bearing on his cognitive development as well as on the type of
communication in which he can engage, the student's school career
might well seem to be programmed even before he is tracked
through elementary and high schools. Discussing the educational
situation in France, M. Gilly argues that "the most important reason for differential success is certainly related to the different intellectual levels of the children. These levels depend directly on
the cultural equipment of their parents. . . . The poverty of the
language spoken at home is one of the most important factors
behind the educational difficulties of children . . . because the
curriculum provided by the school is essentially verbal." [83]
Since the language of educational institutions constitutes the
codified culture of any society and since the messages transmitted
are pieces of information students are meant to comprehend, an
inability to decode that language would necessarily lead to educational retardation. The culture embodied by educational in-

stitutions is that of the dominant groups or class. Any de facto exclusion of members of the lower classes from this culture restricts strategic elites to those who are born into the strata that have created that culture. In this process of selection, educational institutions play a crucial role because in this manner they can perpetuate and legitimate the class structure. By institutionalizing the cultural hegemony of the middle and upper classes, the stratification structure can, in a so-called open society, reproduce itself in an acceptable manner.[84] If educational institutions do not provide members of the lower classes with the cognitive and linguistic tools necessary for high status positions, a certain equilibrium between supply and demand in the job market will be guaranteed. When demand exceeds supply, higher educational institutions become accessible to lower-class members. This "democratization" seems, however, to be concentrated in technical fields. That higher education serves, for the most part, the upper-middle and upper classes is a phenomenon observable in both capitalist and socialist societies.*

There is no question that today the number of lower-class students in universities is higher than it was in the beginning of this century. However, compared with the number of students coming from the middle and upper classes, the proportion of lower-class students is still quite small. Both in France and in Germany the working class constitutes about 50 per cent of the population.[86] In 1963, only 8.7 per cent of the French university students and 5.9 per cent of the German university students were of working-class origin.[87] Although professionals (individuals in *les professions liberales*) accounted for 5.1 per cent of the French population in 1963, their children made up 28.8 per cent of the university population.[88] Lower-class students who have succeeded

---

* In Hungary, for example, 34 per cent of the upper-middle-class children attended universities in 1963 as compared to 7 per cent of the working-class children. Sixty-nine per cent of the upper-middle-class children remained in the upper-middle and middle classes. Seventy per cent of the children of skilled workers remained in the working class and only 3 per cent succeeded in joining the upper-middle class.[85]

in entering and graduating from academic high schools have free access to higher education, which as a public institution in both countries presents fewer economic obstacles than, say, higher education in the United States. However, these students tend to fail more often than middle-class students and are especially weak in the humanities, that is, those areas which are culturally most alien.[89]

In both academic high schools and universities an "overselection principle" tends to operate which ensures that only the best of the working-class students will survive. Apart from the cultural disadvantages with which the lower-class student has to cope, there is an institutional prejudice against which he or she must struggle. A working-class student with above average intellectual ability will be subject to rigorous scrutiny and a bias that favors, even if unconsciously, middle-class mannerisms and comportment. A middle-class student of comparable ability often can get by since he is not expected to demonstrate time and again that he is gifted and merits a bourgeois benediction.

In German academic high schools (*Gymnasium*) during the early sixties, the proportion of working-class students decreased from 20.3 per cent in the entrance class to 8.5 per cent in the graduating classes. In the same period, 43 per cent of French university students from the working class abandoned their studies, whereas 32 per cent of those coming from white-collar groups left prematurely, and 29 per cent of the upper-middle- and upper-class students did so.[90] In the United States, class-specific success rates were most vividly demonstrated in the college system of the City of New York after an open admissions policy was institutionalized in 1971. The dropout rate for freshmen doubled—in part because most of the open admission students came from the lower classes.[91]

American lower-class students labor under a cultural handicap even though this country is not characterized by the sharp cultural differentiation along class lines that can be observed in France and Great Britain. S. Bowles reported data which clearly indicate that lower-class students' chance of getting a college education in the midsixties was more limited than that of students from higher socioeconomic strata, even in cases where there were no differences in the students' respective academic abilities. In addition, Bowles' data indicated that lower-class students who ranked more than one quartile higher in their academic aptitudes than upper-middle-class students were still less likely to obtain a college education.[92]

One of the factors contributing to class-specific success rates is the intelligence quotient which has been shown to be related to language, family structure, and family size.[93] The positive correlation between I.Q. and socioeconomic status has been estimated to be in the range of 0.3 to 0.5.[94] The mean I.Q. difference between upper-middle and working-class children varies between 13 and 21 points.[95] It has been sufficiently demonstrated that I.Q. tests are biased in favor of the verbal middle-class culture, discriminating against children from the lower classes.

Past attempts to restructure educational institutions in order to provide more opportunity for the lower classes have had limited success. In England an educational reform act was passed in 1944. The evidence indicates that the lower-middle class profited from the reform, but the working class did not.[96] The same holds true for France where the democratization of the universities in the late 1940's largely served lower-middle-class students.[97] There are strong indications that the open admission policy in the New York City college system has been most beneficial, not for the groups to which open admission was addressed, namely, the black and Puerto Rican communities, but for students of white upper-lower- or lower-middle-class status. It is not surprising that the broadening of the university population benefits the lower-middle class since this class does not share a specific language code and its linguistic patterns and socialization techniques usually contain elements from both higher and lower classes. Members of the lower-middle class can therefore more easily adjust to the culture and langauge of the higher strata.

The Coleman report, the most comprehensive analysis of social factors influencing American education undertaken to date, demonstrated that equal educational opportunity is a goal which cannot be attained as long as divergent social conditions persist. Coleman corroborates the proposition that family background is of overriding importance which, at this time, cannot be offset by any specific educational program. Subsequent studies and a reanalysis of Coleman's data confirmed his original findings.[98]

Remedial programs which stop short of resocialization to effect both motivational patterns and language performance seem doomed to failure. Regina Reichwein, in an effort to overcome the cultural differences between student and teacher, has suggested the use of an entirely new mode of communication in the classroom. The teacher would no longer rely on verbal explanations in his elaborated code in order to introduce lower-class students to abstract reasoning. Rather he would use the formalized language of new math (set theory) through which the student would become familiar with relations, functions, and levels of abstractions.* But in the final analysis, possibilities of democratizing educational institutions are limited unless drastic measures are taken such as the introduction of a quota system permitting only a specified percentage of middle- and upper-class students to pursue higher education.* *

Whatever is taught in educational institutions in some way contributes to the formation of the citizen. In a society with demo-

---

* Though the study was confined to students taking math courses, Reichwein suggests that "children whose cognitive structure has been constrained by their "restricted" linguistic structure will thus newly acquire those early thought processes that are internalized by a child born to parents with an elaborated language code and raised by help of the emotive and cognitive categories inherent in that code." [99]
* * In the early fifties half of all students admitted to universities in East Germany had to be of peasant or working-class origin, even if better qualified middle-class students applied. Because of this quota system, a high proportion of the children of the upper-middle and old upper class was not admitted to the university, and for that reason a great many professionals and their families left East Germany.

cratic structures, the goal of civic education is to make it possible for each citizen to participate in the body politic. Ideally the student learns to understand the political context of his society and to recognize existing conflicts and problems. Thus children who come from a background where the parents are politically apathetic or have little knowledge about the society in which they are living could acquire at school the comprehension and values necessary to evaluate the political system. This type of education presupposes that those who teach provide accurate knowledge of given political institutions, that they examine alternative interpretations of society, and that they encourage serious thinking about politics and societal problems. The picture that emerges from Hess's and Torney's study of the elementary school is quite the opposite. In the early sixties Robert Hess and Judith Torney observed in their study of schools totaling more than 12,000 elementary school children in the United States

compliance to rules and authority is the major focus of civics education in elementary schools. . . . Teachers of young children place particular stress upon citizen compliance, de-emphasizing all other topics. The three items rated as more important than basic subjects (reading and arithmetic) by a majority of second- and third-grade teachers were *the law, the policeman,* and *the child's obligation to conform* to school rules and the laws of the community. . . . Political socialization at early age levels emphasizes behavior that relates the child emotionally to his country and impresses upon him the necessity for obedience and conformity. . . . The tendency to evade some realities of political life seems to be paralleled by the school's emphasis upon compliance.[100]

Reaction to this type of education is far from uniform. According to the above study, "high status children and high I.Q. children perceive laws as less rigid than do low status children. . . . [They] saw the compliance system in less absolute terms, recognizing the possibility that laws may be defective even though they must be obeyed." [101]

The slant of textbooks most commonly used for civic education and social studies corresponds to the attitudes described above.

According to J. P. Shaver, civil disobedience, dissent, and non-conformity are often treated as undesirable aspects of the community, and political value conflicts are not discussed.[102] One study by E. Litt found that schools located in working-class communities were oriented to an idealistic and passive view of the political process, transmitting an image of political harmony, whereas schools located in upper-middle-class communities were more oriented toward the examination of political conflicts and an active view of the political process.[103]

It is conceivable that colleges and universities could contribute to the development of students' political sensibilities. The curriculum of schools might be analyzed according to the extent to which it serves either demands of the economic sector of society or critical reflection and the pursuit of knowledge for its own sake. At one end of the continuum we would find educational institutions which have become a force of production proper; at the other, institutions which are communities of scholars. Obviously neither type exists in a pure form, but the proportion of critical as opposed to pragmatic learning is of crucial importance. In educational institutions, the potential for sociopolitical analysis would then be related negatively to the degree of instrumentality and implicit reification of knowledge transmitted and positively to the degree of independence of the knowledge from political and economic interests. If educational language becomes one dimensional in serving only to legitimate existing institutions and to transmit practical-applied knowledge, political reflection ceases.

Prior to the emergence of the industrial sector as the paramount force in Western society, the university had the function of providing interpretational schemes of society in addition to professional training in the traditional fields like law and theology.[104] The technical and pragmatic components of higher education were embedded in a cultural framework, and education that was restricted solely to preparation for a vocation was considered antithetical to the development of the full human being. Thus the student's knowledge was rarely confined to one specific dis-

cipline. Before the intervention of the state into higher education, as demonstrated by the establishment of professional schools
by Napoleon, the university existed as an independent entity, a
supreme but separate manifestation of society's culture. The
classical education provided by academic high schools combined
with the *studium generale* on the university level potentially allowed the student to acquire a broad cultural framework.

Apart from the skills required for the future profession of the
student (if he intended to pursue one), the knowledge and interpretations with which high school and college students were
confronted had a low level of instrumentality. In Europe, the
pragmatic applications of this type of education were so limited
that there was much hostility to it by the developing working-
class movement, the representatives of which demanded toward
the end of the nineteenth century a strictly vocational curriculum.[105]

In America, professional schools as well as religious colleges and
elite universities posited the spiritual formation of man as the ultimate goal of higher education until the middle of the nineteenth
century. The rapid growth of the industrial sector combined with
the growing intervention of private economic interests, as represented by wealthy individuals and foundations, into university
matters resulted in a gradual redefinition of the orientation of
higher education and ultimately in the incorporation of higher
education into the production process. The foundations for such
reorientation in the United States were laid by the Morrill Act
of 1862 that provided federal support for "learning . . . related
to agriculture and the mechanic arts." Many institutions of
learning were established which responded solely to economic
needs without any pretense of providing humanistic or theological
instruction or of serving as finishing schools for gentlemen. The
American system of higher education experienced a process of
pragmatic differentiation and specialization that was—and still is—
unparallelled in Europe.

The purpose of the university in advanced industrial society has not been clearly defined by educators and administrators. In the United States there is no integrating educational philosophy, and higher education is a disoriented and often contradictory process that simultaneously serves the needs of graduate schools and the demands for vocational training. Faced with the attempt to reconcile the students' quest for instant relevance, an organized faculty's interest in occupational security, and political pressures from state or federal funding agencies, colleges are confronted with a crisis of institutional identity.

As the debates in Europe and the United States on the purpose of the university indicate, the only explicit demand made upon the university is the fulfillment of manpower needs of the economic order. Bidimensional education incorporating professional training and, as Jürgen Habermas put it, "the interpretation of the cultural heritage of society . . . [and] the formation of a political consciousness" seems to be on the wane.[106] Reforms in the universities of Europe and the United States are transforming them into advanced vocational schools which proffer technical skills and knowledge. In the United States these changes are encouraged by a belief in mass education which, according to Hofstadter's analysis of education in America, is based not upon a "passion for the development of the mind or upon pride in learning and culture for their own sakes, but rather upon the supposed political and economic benefits of education." [107] These goals, the production of scientific and technical knowledge which can be applied to industrial or administrative objectives, combined with financial dependence on outside forces increasingly define the nature of education.

Since education as a quest for truth and emancipation remains alien to most current institutions of higher learning, the lower-class student who tends to study technical subjects has no access to a range of symbols which would allow him to gain distance from society, to critically analyze his environment, and to understand individual difficulties as problems fermenting within the social or political cauldron. Political reflection does not of course automatically spring from a liberal arts curriculum, but it can be argued that the nineteenth century university student was more likely inspired to ponder the values or structure of his society after reading Thomas More's *Utopia* or Rousseau's *Social Contract* than today's working-class student studying Shannon's laws of thermodynamics.

Only disciplines within the humanities or the social sciences still allow the student to gain an over-all view of society since these areas are not yet bound to the demands of the production process. They provide interpretations which lend themselves to an analysis of society. Students in these fields can perceive and articulate conflict zones since they become acquainted, to varying degrees, with ideas that are unhampered by technical and pragmatic considerations.* Their practical experience and their research of social and political problems makes them familiar with the tensions and contradictions of advanced industrial society which they can examine in their sociological, philosophical, or historical contexts. Such emancipatory education is, however, disappearing. The dissolution of liberal arts departments in English provincial universities, recent attempts to reduce the number of sociology students in France and Germany, and the efforts to dilute the liberal arts curricula in American colleges are indications of the direction higher education is taking. That such increased specialization may be dysfunctional for an economy where practical knowledge rapidly becomes obsolete has not been sufficiently taken into account by university reformers.

There is no question that the expansion of higher education is of benefit to those lower-class students who do graduate. This benefit is, however, based solely on an expected increase in one's standard of living. It is not equivalent to political emancipation or to the expansion of individual awareness. It could be concluded

---

* Teachers of the social sciences tend to have liberal political orientations when compared with the instructional staff in the applied arts such as business, engineering, and agriculture. Among the social scientists, sociologists tend to have a left-liberal position.[108]

that, for the most part, colleges and universities do not provide the student coming from the lower classes, or for that matter, any student, with the knowledge and motivation necessary to overcome conformist or apathetic values internalized during childhood. On the contrary, schools which have a predominantly lower-class population reinforce a static image of society and the view that the individual is relatively powerless, a "reed"—not even a "thinking one"—in a forest of overwhelming institutions. In this sense, neither secondary nor higher education is politically innovative; influence on students is neutralized by their basic orientation and does not catalyze their ability to be creatively critical of the society in which they are living.

Participation in political interaction can be distorted by the imposition of official interpretations or the institutionalization of directed communication. If the distortion of communication is effective, demands which threaten the stability of the system can no longer be articulated. In the advanced capitalistic societies, however, the stability of the political system cannot be attributed to directed communication or overt manipulation of the public.

Rather, stability seems to be linked to distortions of political communication which are related to the social structure insofar as it is expressed in class-specific language codes and socialization patterns, as well as to constraints on public communication, which will be discussed in the next chapter. Because of the restricted language code and rigid socialization patterns, the individual from the lower classes engages in arrested communication and tends to see the political universe as a static one and to abide by the prescriptions of external authorities. The impact of primary socialization is such that it can be overcome only with great difficulty. For the most part, educational institutions do not provide individuals with the tools necessary for an active view of political issues, and even where this is attempted it has little effect on those well socialized at home to a passive political perspective.

In the middle classes an elaborated language code and flexible person-oriented socialization techniques make for a self-differentiated individual whose linguistic and cognitive abilities and sense of autonomy allow for reflection upon political institutions. Such a person can consciously choose to support or oppose the political system and articulate interests other than those which are predefined. His ability to handle symbols and his consciousness, which can be verbalized, enable him to comprehend policies and institutions with which he is confronted and be cognizant of the problems his society is facing.

The analysis here, restricted so far to elements of socialization and language, would indicate that the lower classes tend to be the principal scaffolding of existing institutions in advanced industrial society and that the middle classes appear as those who could potentially articulate alternatives to the political and institutional status quo. To what extent these predispositions are translated into actual support of or opposition to the prevailing political system can be shown only in an analysis of the effectiveness of ideologies and governmental claims to legitimacy in advanced industrial society.

3

THE MAINTENANCE
OF THE STATUS QUO

An anomaly of Western industrial society is that social disparities persist amidst plenty while the structure of domination remains virtually unchallenged. Domination, used in this sense, is the control by a limited and relatively small number of people over the allocation of resources and the access to significant participation in the decision-making process. The following discussion will deal with several factors which permit the continuation of existing institutional arrangements and economic stratification, with particular emphasis on constraints of public communication. This analysis of the status quo will also take into account the crucial role played by collective beliefs, which provide the evaluative dimension in communication, the position of the working class vis-à-vis change and political communication, and the influence of both governmental structures and economic imperatives on public communication. This chapter and the following one will draw largely from material dealing with the United States.

CONSTRAINED COMMUNICATION

Conformity to a political system may best be described as the unquestioning acceptance of dominant institutions that determine the quality of life of the society as a whole. Both directed and arrested communication are distortions of political communication in that they prevent individuals and groups from articulating their interests. They are not, however, the only factors which prevent this articulation. Although there hardly exists absolute knowledge in the sense of ultimate political theories and concepts independent of time and space, there are at each point in societal development explanatory concepts which allow for a political understanding of society. Constrained communication, that is, communication between the government and the public and public communication regarding societal problems which are subject to the systematic bias of governmental and private interests, makes such an understanding difficult to achieve. Constrained communication is, of course, either reinforced or modified by the ability to conceptualize and the language code of a group or an individual.

Political Communication and System Maintenance

Political interpretations are influenced by the withdrawal of information and the dissemination of rationalizations which are not meant to become apparent to the public. Policies, explanations, and data can be couched in a language which itself contains predefinitions and interpretations that serve the purpose of maintaining an undisturbed exercise of political power. If the members of a political community are not significantly involved in the decision-making process and if they do not dispose of sufficient sociopolitical knowledge as well as a language that facilitates the unscrambling of governmental jargon and expository style often designed to disguise intent, they have no counterinterpretations to offset official ones, nor can they establish relationships among fragmented pieces of political information they may obtain through the mass media.

Basic societal problems can be camouflaged by the dominant

groups* which occupy or influence positions of political authority and therefore are not subject to political debate unless they cause overt disruption of such proportions that defy concealment. It does not serve the interests of any government to propagate the ills of a society. This is a task left to those who seek election to public office, to journalists and social scientists, and to the groups which experience the social or economic consequences of societal problems.

In advanced industrial society, information has become a crucial prerequisite for both political control and opposition politics, a necessity which is due to factors such as the complexity of society, the growth of governmental bureaucracies, and the tremendous distance between those who make the decisions and the individual citizen. Even though the mass media and the growing literacy of the population create the preconditions for an informed public, it could be argued that the political information the individual possesses decreases in proportion to the total information that exists, much of which is reposited with governmental agencies. The limited knowledge of contemporary society that can be acquired through educational institutions in addition to governmental constraints on communication leave most of the public ignorant of the mechanisms of the decision-making process and the forces influencing it. Unfamiliarity with the facts and arguments considered in political decisions and policy formation results in a reluctance to evaluate governmental actions, especially if they do not seem to have a bearing on everyday life.

Probably no social scientist would dispute the contention that governmental restrictions on public debate are prevalent in modern politics. These constraints became even more evident under the Nixon administration during which civil servants refused, on executive order, to testify before a congressional hearing inves-

---

* The term "dominant group" will be used to denote that minority of individuals which controls the decision-making process. Beyond the group's unifying interest of preserving the structures of domination and an unchanged economic system, the policies of that group are not uniform since different segments of the group are motivated by the goal of maximizing their particular interests. These segments will be designated by the plural, "dominant groups."

tigating foreign policy. Further insulating the presidency from the public, Nixon invoked executive privilege to withhold information from the Senate Foreign Relations Committee and condoned the systematic obstruction of the Watergate investigation. Inquiry into governmental policies was also restricted by the Supreme Court decisions of 1972 that removed congressional immunity to grand jury investigation and that denied journalists the right to use the first amendment in order to protect their sources of information. Though deciding against Nixon in the Watergate case, the same court significantly expanded Presidential power to control political communication by ruling in July 1974 that there is a constitutional basis for a privilege for Presidential communication. By making new law, the court provided future Presidents with a constitutional basis for the invocation of executive privilege.*

The purpose and policies of constrained communication were candidly stated by Justice Lewis F. Powell, two months prior to his appointment to the Supreme Court by Nixon, in a confidential memorandum that was circulated by the United States Chamber of Commerce among high echelons in the business community. It was recommended in this memorandum that individuals and groups with opposing or critical views of American business should be "penalized politically," businessmen should influence universities for reasons of "balancing" faculties, and textbooks should be "evaluated" as part of an all-out effort in which "the wisdom, ingenuity and resources of American business [ought] to be marshaled against those who would destroy it." Television programs "should be monitored in the same way that textbooks should be kept under constant surveillance. This applies not merely to so-called educational programs . . . but to the daily 'news analysis' which so often includes the most insidious type of criticism of the enterprise system." [2]

Grand jury proceedings against publishers and writers, White House efforts to block legislation expanding the Freedom of Information Act, and President Ford's refusal to make C.I.A. records

---

* The only exception referred to in the Supreme Court decision are criminal proceedings. "The generalized assertion of privilege must yield to the demonstrated specific need for evidence in a pending criminal case."[1]

available to the Senate Committee on Intelligence are overt governmental attempts to infringe upon the public's right to know.*[3] A complete understanding of governmental policy is made difficult if not impossible if information regrading political decisions is withheld or deliberately beclouded. Nor will history necessarily be able to unravel the snare. As one official investigation into the decision-making process revealed, the manner in which important decisions are arrived at frequently cannot be reconstructed, simply because written records do not exist for all stages of the process. Such was the lesson of the *Pentagon Papers*.[5] "The Pentagon researchers generally lacked records of the oral discussions of the National Security Council or the most intimate gatherings of the Presidents with their closest advisers, where decisions were often reached." But the leakage of this document about American involvement in Vietnam also indicates the limits of governmental constraints on communication. The total compliance of civil servants, consultants, and politicians involved in the formulation and execution of policy is critical in order to keep the public uninformed. Because civil servants have refused to remain silent, the attention of the public has been drawn during the last few years to a number of issues such as the corruption of civil servants and elected politicians and the surveillance of civilians by the army and other governmental agencies.[6] The ignorance of large segments of the public of pertinent information and paradigms excludes them from effective political communication. This limited use of communication is beneficial for the interests of dominant groups since the less people know, the easier it is to govern them and thereby achieve ends which may not have the consent of a significant portion of the population. An individual may respond to his lack of knowledge about politics with what Hannah Arendt calls the privatization of meaning. When sociopolitical reality is relentlessly obfuscated by official incantations, the indi-

---

* Not to speak of the C.I.A.'s censoring of books and undercover financing of several books published by Praeger.[4]

vidual withdraws, in surrender, from politics and ceases to participate in political communication.

The obfuscation of political reality can be achieved with the use of a highly evocative, ritualistic language.[7] Political campaigns and careers are dependent upon symbolic, rhetoric-laden statements which have little if any effect on the decision-making process. Elected and appointed officials may agree publicly with abstract demands for equality and better education for the poor and rush to microphones and cameras when an emotional issue such as the state of mental institutions has caught public attention never to be heard of again after public interest and the commercial gain of the media from the issue have been exhausted. Politicians trumpet their concern about rising prices and crime in the street, stage public hearings, and listen to the voice of the common man. The public is—and probably wants to be—reassured by political symbolism of its civic importance while the decision-making process itself runs counter to its interests. Regulatory agencies respond to that desire by engaging in public impression management while they serve the very economic interests they are meant to regulate.[8] It seems that the more often the public interest is invoked by politicians and government officials the less often such rhetoric has any consequences.

One of the functions of constrained communication is that office holders retain control over the management of public issues. Moynihan's suggestion that the government limit public statements about poverty and racism reflects the principle that nothing should be transformed into a political issue that cannot be accommodated within the existing political framework. Put differently, issues which challenge dominant private and governmental interests must become nonissues and must be kept as such. If that attempt fails, the problem is to be given token recognition.

In his critique of the pluralistic orientation in political science which systematically disregards the existence of nonissues and the structural constraints of political communication, Kenneth Dolbeare has pointed out that "established institutions and processes permit only certain relatively congenial pressures to be aired, and they repress or label illegitimate all they cannot absorb. By the time an issue reaches the stage of public consideration within the bounds established by these institutions and processes, it has already been hammered into a form that can be accommodated without serious difficulty." [9]

Peter Bachrach and Morton S. Baratz applied the concept "mobilization of bias"* in their analysis of the decision-making process. This phrase describes the process in which "the dominant values and the political myths, rituals, and institutional practices" are mobilized to "favor the vested interests of one or more groups. . . ." [10] Systematic bias in political communication suspends the articulation of those issues which would require a change in the orientation of existing policies or in the present allocation of benefits and privileges. These issues are therefore "suffocated . . . kept covert; or killed before they gain access to the relevant decision making arena." [11] If subordinate groups do not possess the knowledge and material and organizational resources that are strategically necessary for the pursuit of their goals, they can be disregarded. The bias of the political process rarely becomes evident because the nature of public controversy is shaped in advance by the elites and because "power utilized in this form is usually exercized covertly, far removed from the glare of the public." [12]

Structured Consensus

Just as the suppression of public issues delimits the parameter of political communication so does a structured consensus. A structured consensus is either one which is reached by political elites and passed down to the public that responds as an acclamatory agent only, or one which is formulated according to the imperatives of the political–economic system. There is obviously a close re-

---

* The concept was developed by E. E. Schattschneider in *The Semisovereign People* (New York: Holt, Rinehart and Winston, 1960).

lation between the two types of structured consensus, as the elite consensus is often influenced by the imperatives of system maintenance. Nevertheless it is necessary to separate the two types analytically because the second type that is tied to system maintenance imperatives may induce a consensus independent of group or class interests that are the core of the first type of structured consensus. Interest in economic growth is, for example, shared by trade unionists and property holders alike, even though its benefits are distributed unequally.

There is no question that the foremost determinant of the structured consensus is the necessity to sustain economic growth, a necessity which takes precedent over all other system requirements. It is essential that economic growth be perpetuated in order to generate enough surplus for the capital needs of the private sector and for governmental operations. Because the political compliance of the population is no longer ensured by an integrating ideology—as will be shown subsequently—continued mass loyalty has to be obtained through material and social compensations, that is, primarily through the fulfillment of consumer demands, the maintenance of a high standard of living, and the promise of even more affluence and leisure to consume even more enticing goods and, secondarily, through the provision of social services such as education, medical care, welfare, and social security. These topics dominate political communication in advanced industrial societies. What is significant about the economic constraint that structures consensus and distorts communication is that issues that cannot be tied to the goal of production and increased revenues will not be considered seriously. The system requirement of economic growth adumbrates all areas of decision making and is a theme that will reappear throughout the following chapter.

In his work *Consent and Consensus*, Percy H. Partridge wrote that "some components of the prevailing consensus on which the system depends will be the products of pressures exerted by dominant institutions and elites: the system itself plays a part in the manufacture of attitudes and habits required for its own survival.

Elements of consensus are implanted and consolidated by the downward pressures of institutional practice." [13] If one follows that perspective, consensus is understood as descending from the top instead of ascending from the bottom. Structural mechanisms rather than the public determine the orientation and direction of political communication. This obviously does not mean that there are no areas left that are susceptible to the public will. But whatever is left to public discretion is secondary, having no long-range societal consequences. Capital punishment, abortion, or state aid to parochial schools appear insignificant as issues when compared with the initial decision of committing American forces to Vietnam.

It follows the logic of the interest in system maintenance that public debate about secondary issues is encouraged since it deflects attention from crucial issues and creates the illusion of participation in the political process. As long as important segments of the public believe in democratic principles, this illusion has to be perpetuated in order to preclude dissatisfaction and sustain loyalty. The political and economic imperatives of system stability establish a range of priorities and goals which decide the substance of a manufactured consensus. The task of governmental elites is the implementation of these goals rather than the questioning of goals or priorities.

When the above imperatives of system maintenance and the interests of the dominant groups are taken into account, it becomes apparent that constrained communication and the transformation of consensus into "a product of, rather than a condition for, a political system of domination" [14] creates a communicative framework which structurally excludes feedback from the public and ruptures the liberal notion of the public as a countervailing force to those in power. Although structured consensus is linked to political imperatives and interests, there are, however, other constraints that are engendered by social structures which also distort political communication.

Language as Noise

Groups which share a restricted speech code unwittingly contribute to the objective of constrained communication because their linguistic patterns introduce "noise" or distortion into communication. The preceding chapter demonstrated the existence of arrested communication among large segments of the population as evidenced in a restricted language code which, it is suggested acts as a barrier to political communication. Language is a distorting factor when it impedes the acquisition of information and when it introduces noise into the process of communication. In highly organized and differentiated societies, a considerable amount of sociopolitical knowledge and communicative competence is required for effective participation in political communication. Groups and individuals who have internalized and are thus bound by a restricted language code cannot cope with sophisticated messages nor effectively comprehend a complex political environment.

That language can interfere in communication can be shown in an analysis of the transmission of information through the media. As a source of information and interpretations, the media are increasingly important in political communication and form, what is for the most part, a precarious link between the individual and all the governmental, quasigovernmental, and private institutions which constitute the dominant forces in his society.

According to communication theory, there is no transmission of information without some loss of information. In most cases this loss results from the nature of the channel used for the transmission of information. But it is also due to entropy or loss of information stemming from human factors as studies of retention capacity and attention span show. The further possibility that information can be lost for linguistic reasons has not frequently been a topic of empirical research. Because language is a communicative instrument used for the transmission of thoughts, messages, and information, it can be analyzed as a source of noise in two capacities: as a channel (syntax, conceptual framework) and as a medium (vocabulary). If the channel is not intricate enough for the transmission or reception of complex messages, noise is generated and information will be lost. A language without a conditional mode or prepositional constructions, for example, is adequate to communicate only the most rudimentary thoughts. As a medium, language can be a source of noise if the lexical differentiation that is necessary for the transmission and reception of qualified messages is missing. The quality of both medium and the channel directly affects the quality of the communication.

The following simplified model may serve to illustrate potential loss of information: From a general situation (1), a specific event is chosen by a news medium (2). In the encoding process (the code being defined by the social referents and interpretation framework of the encoder), the event is translated into a message (3). The message, consisting of a definite number of bits of information, passes through a channel where it is transformed into signals (4) the form of which is determined by the type of medium chosen (television, radio, periodicals). The signals arrive at the receiver (5) who reconstitutes them as a message (6) and decodes it according to his framework of interpretation (7).

Since a loss of information can occur during each stage of the process, the net result of the transmission is in all likelihood a refracted understanding. A specific event among many possible ones is chosen, the context of which cannot always be re-established during the reception of the message. In the process of encoding, an interpretation within a given framework is imposed on the event. Technical factors cause the loss of information during the transmission. In the decoding stage, the message is filtered through the semantic and ideational code of the receiver.

The processes of encoding and decoding are influenced by sociolinguistic as well as interpretational factors. If the receiver is confronted with complex messages which are communicated in terms unknown to him, he will most likely scan the message only very superficially. If he continues to listen to the message he may apply an interpretation far different from the one used by the commentator, provided that the receiver considers the message to be relevant and disposes of an interpretational framework. A message encoded as "students demand participation" will be decoded according to the receiver's linguistic code and interpretational framework. Those sharing the restricted code may not be able to translate participation into something meaningful and retain only those elements of the message which are secondary. If the message is transmitted against the visual background of an occupied campus building, the restricted code speaker will probably understand it in terms of student unrest per se instead of what the unrest is inspired by or directed toward.

A different response is likely for groups sharing the elaborated code. The message does not pose a semantic problem as far as the meaning of the term nor a syntactic one as far the qualifications employed are concerned. Moreover, the issue of participation is closer to the dominant values of the elaborated code speaker than it is to those of restricted code speakers. It is obvious that an understanding of the message does not necessarily imply an agreement with the particular demand contained in this message, though any agreement or disagreement is contingent upon an understanding of the concept. Information can also be lost, or more precisely disregarded, if the framework of interpretation used for the message by the transmitter contradicts the interpretational rules used by the receiver.

The Influence of the Media

A number of other factors govern the transmission and reception of messages. It is clear that any medium, whether television, radio, or periodicals which generates too much noise in the transmission of information will be in perpetual search of an audience and that such a situation is the exception rather than the rule. In most cases there is a correspondence between the sophistication of a medium—with respect to language and interpretations—and that of the audience. An analysis of the *Daily News* and the *New York Times* by James Chambers showed significant differences between the two papers in the use of syntax and vocabulary.[15] The simplified wording and sentences of the *Daily News* correlated, as would be expected, with the class background of its readership which tends toward a restricted code, while the more complex vocabulary and syntax of the *New York Times* corresponded to the generally elaborated code of its middle-class readers. Research on a German mass circulation paper, the *Bildzeitung*, corroborates Chambers's analysis. Ekkehart Mittelberg found a number of stylistic elements in this German paper which are typical of the restricted code, such as concrete metaphors, dichotomized statements, simplified sentence structures, typified formulations, an undifferentiated vocabulary, and stereotypifications.[16] The use of a restricted code by these papers results in unqualified descriptions of political reality which more often than not are conservatively slanted. Because of the style utilized, the reader's language does not inhibit comprehension, but he may be manipulated through the effective application of the very stereotypes which he uses in his everyday language. As Mittelberg suggested, an appeal to emotions, strong metaphors, and superficial formulations suspend the reader's thinking.[17] The frame of reference of these papers is consistent, and it is possible to predict with a high degree of accuracy their interpretations of a given political event. Sensationalism, repetition, and a simplistic depiction of political reality contribute little to the readers' knowledge of society.

Other observers of media addressed to both lower- and middle-class groups have come up with similar findings. The French philosopher and sociologist Henri Lefebvre remarked that the "mass media form the taste and dilute judgement. They instruct and they condition. They fascinate and they debase by saturation with images, with 'news' that is not newsworthy. They proliferate communication and threaten coherence and reflection, vocabulary and verbal expression, and language itself."* [18]

Editorial policies in the mass media cannot be detached from commercial considerations which require that the largest possible audience be reached. Interpretations which may alienate either the sponsor or the audience of a program generally will not be transmitted. In early 1972 David W. Rintels, chairman of the Committee on Censorship of the Writers Guild of America, testified before the Senate Subcommittee on Constitutional Rights that, according to a poll of the Guild, of those who responded

eighty-six per cent have found, from *personal* experience, that censorship exists in television. Many state, further, that they have never written a script, no matter how innocent, that has not been censored. Eighty-one per cent believe that television is presenting a distorted picture of what is happening in this country today—politically, economically and racially. Only eight per cent believe that current television programming is "in the public interest, convenience and necessity" as required by the Federal Communications Act of 1934.[20]

This censorship is exerted prior to and during the production of a program not only by the sponsor but also by companies that invest heavily in television advertising. This was the case in the spring of 1972 when the National Broadcasting Company removed a section from a documentary on the conditions of migrant workers employed by a Florida subsidiary of the Coca-Cola Company because of pressures applied by the parent corporation.[21]

The "dramatic, low taste content" of entertainment is most likely to appeal to the majority of the consumers who are little educated and who do not critically evaluate the programs they watch or hear.[22] Programming corresponds for the most part to the

---

* If the receiver of a message has doubts about its content, it will be repeated since redundancy "is the simplest way of reducing the equivocation [of] the receiver." Persuasion calls for repetition and the reduction of complex matters into a limited number of typifications and their associated negative or positive connotations.[19]

tastes and preferences of the audience and serves to "maintain the
financial equilibrium of a deeply institutionalized social system
[the media] which is tightly integrated with the whole of the
American economic institutions." [23] This function of the media
deflects public attention from political issues and perpetuates the
definition of the "good life" in strictly materialistic terms.

Though the audience may influence the type of entertainment
presented in the media, it has little control over the selection of
information and quality of interpretations transmitted. The flow
of information is downward as is the direction of influence.[24]
Certainly, the individual can disregard a message because he deems
it irrelevant or incorrect. But the validity of political messages,
such as those pertaining to foreign and fiscal policies, cannot be
assessed at the moment of transmission, since any evaluation presupposes an acquaintance with the relevant facts most of the
audience does not have.

It is precisely in this area where the stabilizing influence of the
media becomes apparent. As noted in Chapter 2, individuals belonging to the lower classes are more dependent on group norms
than those coming from the middle classes. Conformity and
allegiance to established authority as well as resistance to change
were found to be political predispositions of individuals brought
up in the lower classes. Empirical research also demonstrates that
class-specific factors such as conformity, reception to one-sided
arguments, and the absence of skepticism correlate with the susceptibility to persuasion and manipulation.[25] Influence of interpretations and opinions disseminated by the media on large
segments of the audience cannot be doubted.

Governmental constraints on political communication, the mobilization of bias by powerful interests, and the commercial character of the media create a situation where news items that would
invite challenges of the status quo are either omitted or embedded in interpretations which depreciate them. If members of
the audience have no counterinterpretations or alternative sources
of information, they may mistake for the real world the selected

messages presented by the media. In doing so they unwittingly support existing institutions and policies. Renate Mayntz has described this condition as the "half-resigned acceptance of the *status quo* [which] may well be reinforced by a fake cultural integration and feeling of participation induced by the mass media." [26]

The proposition that mass media contribute to the reinforcement of existing conditions has to be qualified by reiterating that such a reinforcement is possible only if the messages transmitted correspond to the communicative competence of the audience and if the audience has a framework of interpretation similar to the one used by the media. The latter qualification opens the door for an inquiry into a larger area, namely the collective beliefs and ideologies which shape the interpretation of political messages.

COLLECTIVE BELIEFS:
IDEOLOGIES AND PARA-IDEOLOGIES

The expectations which guide man's political behavior and the manner in which he interprets his condition are structured by values and collective beliefs transmitted in the socialization process. No matter how refracted and irrational these beliefs and values may be, they influence the political positions an individual may take.

Nature and Function of Ideologies

The continuity of collective beliefs, whether they take the form of ideologies, religions, or para-ideologies, is a stabilizing force in any political system. Collective beliefs can express the interests of the dominant group which provides seemingly plausible interpretations of political reality, or they can convey or abet counterinterpretations, usually finding their adherents among groups or classes which do not participate in or benefit from the decision-making process. Ideologies are considered here as integrated belief systems which provide explanations for political reality and establish the collective goals of a class or group, and in the case of a dominant ideology, of society at large. They have an evaluative component in that they attach either negative or positive judgments to conditions in society and to political goals. The normative dimension of an ideology is an essential component without which an ideology could not function effectively. By setting standards of action and priorities, this dimension cements the believer's loyalty to the group, class or society which shares the ideology.

In order that an ideology is accepted by a class or a group, it must translate its economic needs and social aspirations into a coherent structure. An ideology posits a model of the political order which is subjectively plausible to the individual since it validates his interests and position. The success or failure of an ideology is therefore contingent upon the extent to which it makes what people experience in their daily lives comprehensible in political terms. When an ideology is accepted, those who come to adhere to it recognize themselves in that ideology; through it they can express their aspirations and define their political objectives. In such a case an ideology serves to mobilize people.

Any analysis of ideology in the twentieth century has been influenced by Marx's critique of ideologies which clearly established the political function of collective beliefs. Marx and Engels contended that man's consciousness is shaped by the material conditions of his existence. His thoughts, beliefs, and ideological predispositions, they asserted, are not independent of the individual's position in the production process. True, "men are the producers of their conceptions . . . [but] consciousness can never be anything else than conscious existence, and the existence of men is their actual life process. . . . Life is not determined by consciousness but consciousness by life." [27] Man's consciousness is thus a product of his ongoing activities pursued within the confines of his socieconomic condition.

According to this Marxian definition, the division of society into social classes set apart by differing material conditions and life styles gives rise to class-specific beliefs based upon the respective economic interests of these classes. Marx held that all forms of political thought (though not including his own theories) and all ideologies distorted reality since they originated—in the ultimate analysis—in the material interests of one class or another and not in the interests of society as a whole. For Marx, ideologies are understood as systems of misleading ideas based on illusions. Ideology is equated to a consciousness of reality wherein "men and their circumstances appear upside down as in a *camera obscura*." [28] This false consciousness is the erroneous belief that political conceptions are independent of material reality, that is, economic conditions and interests. Claims of independence from class-specific interests are alone proof that ideologies distort political reality.

The dominant ideology of a society reflects, in the Marxian analysis, the interests of the ruling class, whether this ideology is expressed in political theories such as pluralism or conservatism, in the legal framework, or in religious beliefs such as those of feudal Europe or theocratic Geneva. An ideology is "representative of determinate limited interests" which the dominant class pursues. From this perspective the claim of the right to private property is not understood as a natural right but as a right linked to the interests of those who hold property. A dominant ideology is transmitted through educational institutions; if subordinate groups accept it, they will develop a false consciousness since they come to adhere to political conceptions which do not express their own interests. The consciousness of groups and classes is thus shaped by the dominant political belief system and the socioeconomic context in which they are living.*

In Marx's interpretation, a dominant ideology serves to provide interpretations of social reality. It mobilizes groups and classes around the goals and values of society and legitimates the exercise of political domination by suggesting that the existing political structures, and thus the status quo, are the only possible ones.

---

* Marx held that no social group or class is able to formulate nonideological conceptions. According to Karl Mannheim, this task is left to those individuals he called the "unattached intellectuals."

The political perception of the individual is predefined and distorted by a dominant ideology that makes the repression of primary and secondary needs acceptable.

The concept ideology will be used here to designate all politically mobilizing beliefs no matter which group or class adheres to them. All ideologies reflect class- or group-specific interests and differ only in the degrees of distortion of political reality. Dominant ideologies form conceptual foundations which uphold a political system and its institutions. Counterideologies serve to mobilize oppressed groups or classes to oppose the political system. The obvious question is whether in advanced industrial societies dominant ideologies or counterideologies still perform the function they did in the industrial society observed by Marx. Is it possible to understand contemporary political communication using the concept "ideology" and if so, is a dominant ideology generally shared by the population?

If ideologies are understood as belief systems that explain sociopolitical reality and contribute to the cohesion of a society, then it appears unlikely that the majority of the population has a coherent ideological understanding of social and political processes. Today the dominant group invokes less and less frequently traditional ideologies to justify its policies. Nor does it attempt to propagate a new ideology which could function as a dominant one. More significantly, since interpretations offered by an ideology have to correspond to the life experience of the individual, they must be able to integrate and explain new information and new conditions. The rapid change in advanced industrial society would require a constant updating of a dominant ideology, a revision which would in itself alienate the old believers and limit its claim to absolute veracity.

Instead of placing the cause for the decline of ideologies in the attenuation of social conflicts—which could be the expression of a generalized false consciousness—this analysis suggests that the decline is due to the loss of plausibility of traditional ideologies and their interpretations of the political order. Advanced industrial society and newly emerging needs can no longer be grasped within the framework of traditional ideologies. In the liberal ideology, politics is understood as a market place where demands can be fulfilled by means of the purchasing power of the ballot and where laws and legal procedures guarantee equal participation of all. These notions run counter to the political experience of a large proportion of the population. The simultaneous emphasis on distributive justice and the right to private property, particularly in view of the forms and proportions private property has taken in advanced industrial societies, is contradictory. The goals of liberalism, such as the reduction of inequality, may be acceptable to much of the population, but the liberal explanations of the political process and how these goals can be attained are less easily accepted.

The conservative ideology confronts similar difficulties. Less prevalent than the liberal ideology and less often explicit in public policy and legal decisions, the goals and interpretations offered by conservative spokesmen are rarely in harmony with the aspirations or experiences of most of the population. The proposed reduction by the "individualist-conservative" of governmental responsibilities in the economic and social sectors of society and the concomitant emphasis on freedom of choice, individual action, and self-interest are simply contrary to the factual dependency of all groups and classes on the state.[29] "Organic conservatism" which places a greater emphasis on society and authority than on the individual's free choice, postulates that governmental authority should be based on moral principles independent of any group or class interests and considers men as inherently unequal, irrational, and incapable of self-government. In fact, moral principles are rarely applied to political questions. Rather there is the widespread sentiment that those "who have the power are out to take advantage of the population . . . and don't really care what happens to the people." [30] The assumed inherent inequality among men, on the other hand, cannot be reconciled with the quest for social equality by large segments of the population and the democratic ideal of the political equality of all people.

Unlike conservatism and liberalism, socialism (that is, Marxist socialism) claims to have an objective historical basis which can be proven by subjecting social development to scientific examination. However, a number of its predictive statements, like the inevitability of severe economic crises or the absolute pauperization of the working class, have been proven erroneous. Several theoretical and practical problems of socialist ideology are readily apparent. Socialist societies have not been able to reconcile the democratic ideals of their ideology with the demands of a centrally planned economy or to overcome the obstacles to realizing social equality while achieving economic equality. Furthermore, axioms such as the proposition that human labor is the sole source of surplus are questionable in light of the role of science and technology as forces of production. To a great extent, however, the declining plausibility of socialism is due to the experience of totalitarian and bureaucratic communism rather than to problems inherent in the ideology.

If liberalism, conservatism, and socialism are not plausible today, it is in part because the socioeconomic foundations of advanced industrial society are radically different from those of nineteenth century market capitalism during which time these ideologies gained prominence. The nineteenth century saw the birth of the proletariat and the maturation of the bourgeoisie, two classes which provided the social basis for new ideologies. With the possible exception of the ascendence of the upper-middle class over the last decades (a phenomenon that will be discussed in the next chapter), advanced industrial society has not experienced the emergence of a new class on a similar scale. But it would be too facile to explain the declining plausibility of traditional political ideologies as due to simply the development of new economic structures. Mostafa Rejai has enumerated a number of changes within capitalist society that have led to a decline in the intensity of ideological debate. Among these changes are: "an increasing general affluence; an increasing exposure to education and the media of communication; an increasing reliance on science and expertise; an increasing attenuation of class and party conflict; a gradual attainment of political and economic citizenship by the lower classes; a gradual emergence of a vast, homogeneous, professional-managerial middle class; a gradual transformation of laissez-faire capitalism into the welfare state; and a gradual institutionalization of stable political processes for [the] resolution of political issues." [31] In his over-all view of society, Rejai seems to underestimate socioeconomic disparity among social classes and the changes in political configurations proceeding from the economic developments that he notes. Nevertheless, the factors which he singles out, have, by and large, undermined the plausibility of traditional ideologies.

The secondary status of ideologies in contemporary society is evidenced by the absence of empirical research on the subject. Few studies have been executed on the extent to which ideologies are shared by the population, and no research on the question had been conducted in the early decades of this century. Since the origin of ideologies is among intellectuals and since ideologies serve to justify political systems, explicit ideological convictions probably exist only among intellectuals and political elites. As far as the population is concerned, one can assume that there is but a fragmented ideological consciousness. Herbert McClosky's research on the "American democratic ideology" demonstrates that the political consciousness of the active political minority exhibits "by comparison with ordinary voters a more developed sense of ideology and a firmer grasp of its essentials."[32] Angus Campbell observes that variations along the liberal–conservative continuum are applicable to about 15 per cent of the voters and to 12 per cent of the total population. But only 3.5 per cent of the voters and 2.5 per cent of the total population have opinions which could be described as "ideological interpretations of political behavior and political change." [33]

The Emergence of a Para-ideology

As noted above one of the functions of ideologies is the legitimation of domination. Ideologies justify the use of force to maintain the status quo, to initiate social change, and to suppress revolutionary activities. An ideology, if successfully propagated, stabilizes a political system. But when ideology is seen as an integrated system of meaning providing sociopolitical interpretations, the concept has lost much of its usefulness for political analysis. In twentieth century advanced industrial society, an ideology which defends the exercise of political power by a select minority can claim very little adherence either among the dominant group, institutional elites, or the population at large. It therefore is difficult to explain the integration of large segments of the population and specifically of the working class in terms of a false consciousness induced by a dominant ideology. The absence of an integrating ideology poses two questions: First, what substitutes for such an ideology in advanced industrial society; and, second, to what extent is legitimacy and the exercise of authority impaired by the absence of an integrating ideology? The second problem will be dealt with at length in the following chapter.

What is possible to chart in contemporary society that resembles a collective belief system is a generalized acceptance of consumer patterns and a diffuse, abstracted agreement about political institutions. Collective imagery rooted in material and social compensations and slogans of a para-ideological nature have taken over some of the functions of traditional ideologies. Collective images like "the great society," "defense of democracy," "power to the people," "law and order," and "the silent majority" act as substitutes, however pallid, for traditional ideologies.

Historically, the decline of religious value systems was accompanied by a secularization of political ideologies. In advanced industrial society, a justification for the exercise of political power which can embrace both the populace and leaders is not propagated by the ruling group. Instead, one notices the crystallization of a para-ideology which can be understood within the framework of functional rationality. On the surface this para-ideology, which Jürgen Habermas analyzed, though not designating it as such, in his seminal essay, *Technology and Science as "Ideology,"* appears to be independent of class-specific interests and is rooted in the presumed rational administration of a political system.[34] The difference between this para-ideology and traditional ideologies is that it "disconnects legitimating principles from the organization of social life and therefore from social norms of interaction, thus depoliticizing these criteria. Instead they are embedded in the functions of a presumed system of purposive-rational action." [35] Questions of efficiency (or principles of purposive-rational action) rather than of morality dominate decisions. By definition, science and technology, which are part of the system of purposive-rational action, do not provide ethical standards of conduct. For these reasons science and technologies cannot fulfil the spiritual and moral needs of advanced industrial society. Nor do they offer transcendent goals unifying the worker, businessman, and professor. Any "ideology" based on science and technology lacks the normative basis which is an integral part of an ideology; it is a para-ideology only.

The rational administration of society is, according to the para-ideology of science and technology, detached from phenomena such as class conflict or group-specific interests. Habermas argues that "the system justifies itself by achievements which may not, in principle, be interpreted politically. Rather [these achievements] are interpreted directly according to the allocation of money and leisure and indirectly according to the technocratic rationale for excluding practical * [i.e., normative] questions." This allocation is neutral (*verwendungsneutral*) since there are no political norms

* *Praktisch* in Habermas' writing can be understood as a synonym for "normative" or "ethical" and usually refers to questions pertaining to society. The terms "norm" and "normative value" denote a standard of social behavior which the members of a community are expected to adhere to and which can be enforced by sanctions, both positive and negative. Since norms specify how men ought to act, they have moral and evaluative connotations.

regarding the use of money and leisure.[36] Habermas suggests that this system of purposive-rational action increasingly governs the institutions of society, the political framework of which is subverted by purposive-rational thinking that does not take into account the possibility of alternatives either to the existing structure of domination or its policies. Technical rules replace societal norms as guidelines for political action, and rationalization is understood as a process which leads to "the growth of productive forces [and] the expansion of technical-administrative power" instead of "emancipation, individuation, [and] the expansion of domination-free communication." [37]

In the logic of the structured consensus, political debate is shifted from a discussion of ends to one of means, or to put it in Weber's terms, from substantive rationality to functional rationality. Contrary to its claim, this para-ideology cannot be disconnected from class-specific interests. By presenting the given political system as the only possible one, it serves the interests of those groups who profit most from the system. The rationality behind the para-ideology, however, seems to cut across class lines since efficiency, rational administration, and technical rules appear to be at first glance disassociated from any class interest. In fact, a growing importance is being accorded to the role of the expert and scientist. The governmental decision-making process appears depoliticized as technical competence and administrative expertise become key criteria. According to Habermas, the impression is created by this para-ideology that the allocation of resources is independent of values which, however, are always at the base of political decisions. When scientific and technological knowledge are invoked in formulating policies, it becomes more difficult for the population to examine the merits of a decision or to perceive alternatives.

Seymour M. Lipset has made a similar, though less abstract, analysis. He links the declining ideological debate to

the acceptance of scientific thought in matters which have been at the center of political controversy. Insofar as most organized participants [thus the active minority] in the political struggle accept the authority of experts in economics, military affairs, interpretations of the behavior of foreign nations, and the like, it becomes increasingly difficult to challenge the views of opponents on moralistic "either/or" terms. Where there is some consensus among the scientific experts on specific issues, these tend to be removed as possible sources of intense controversy. As the ideology of "scientism" becomes accepted, the ideologies of the extreme left and right lose much of their impact.[38]

The selection of a problem as well as its solution cannot be disconnected from political and social norms.[39] Solicited advice of experts can be disregarded if it does not conform to the political values of the office holders, as Presidential commission reports readily demonstrate, their destiny not infrequently being a library shelf or a locked filing cabinet. And if scientists were in positions of authority, their research and consensus would be influenced as much by normative predispositions as the politicians' are.

To recapitulate, the para-ideology of science and technology makes the exercise of governmental power acceptable by seemingly depoliticizing politics. Scientific and technological knowledge conceal class-specific interests, value systems, and the nature of domination. Because scientific methodologies do indeed develop independently from group or class interests, it is easy to convey implicitly the idea that decision-making based on science and technology is just as detached from special interests. This invocation of scientific methods seriously and deleteriously obscures the political process. The extent to which the para-ideology of science and technology is accepted by the population is unknown, but traces of it can be found in the refracted belief that solutions to social problems can and will eventually be found through scientific research and the application of technological knowledge. Such a belief cements the status quo by de-emphasizing political solutions to society's problems. Compared to traditional ideologies, this para-ideology has little normative power since it provides no ethical criteria. The rationale of efficiency which it embodies is precarious since the efficiency of a policy or an institution can be readily evaluated by the citizen in light of his everyday experience, though it is often documented evaluations of this kind which are the targets of political constraints on communication.

THE INTEGRATION OF THE WORKING CLASS

It would be difficult to maintain the status quo if groups whose cooperation is necessary for the production process did not sanction the status quo either passively or actively. The absence of a dominant ideology and the normative impotence of the para-ideology of science and technology makes such support ever more important. Those segments of the population which are marginal to the process of production are of little political consequence. They find their only means to influence the bargaining process in protest and violence which goes largely unnoticed unless more powerful groups form an alliance with them.[40] To search for the seeds of structural change in the segments of the upper-middle and upper classes that make up the dominant minority would be contradictory since these groups identify with the status quo.* The working class, however, accounts for half of the employed population, and in the United States and in Europe—albeit to different degrees—it is organized into powerful unions.** Because of the functional prerequisite of sustained economic growth of advanced industrial society, a withdrawal of cooperation by the working class would

---

* G. W. Domhoff points out that the basic reorientation of policy in the United States during the depression of the thirties stemmed from realignments in the upper class and that it was a response to a deep economic crisis which threatened to destroy the system.[41] Ever since the thirties, unprecedented economic growth has been interrupted only by periodic recessions. The low probability of severe economic instability, the structured consensus which validates the decision-making process, and vested interests of groups controlling the nation's wealth are all among those factors making for stability.

** Blue-collar, service, and farm workers accounted for 52.1 per cent of the labor force in 1973.[42] Daniel Bell provides the following data on union membership in the United States and in Western Europe:[43]

U.S.A.	22.9%
Great Britain	45.0%
West Germany	close to 40.0%
France	about 20.0%

lead to severe disturbances in the political–economic system. Granted, such a withdrawal is unlikely in light of the communicative patterns and socialization strategies that predominate in these strata, but any proposition about the integration of the working class requires more evidence than that offered so far.

Working-Class Symbolism

Articulated dissent presupposes that political symbols (terms, concepts, and ideological interpretations) be attached to subjectively experienced conditions that do not correspond to expectations or needs. Political consciousness is perforce bound to a symbolic interpretation of sociopolitical experience. The black population in the United States has been living in deprived conditions for centuries. Yet it was not until the early sixties that these conditions were protested on a widespread basis. At that point, the symbols of social justice and equality became part of the political repertoire of liberal upper-middle-class groups and government officials. The actual socioeconomic status could be measured against espoused values. Sources of conflict between lower-class minority groups and dominant political institutions followed from a conscious awareness of economic disparity and unfulfilled expectations regarding the betterment of conditions. As long as no political interpretations were attached to deplorable conditions, these conditions remained inert, posing no threat to the status quo.

An adequate counterideology was available at the time of the working-class struggles of the nineteenth and early twentieth centuries. Terms like profit, exploitation, bourgeoisie, and class had concrete meanings for both workers and intellectuals. These terms allowed the worker to understand the sociopolitical order and to comprehend his subjugation. In the United States the absence of a political party representing labor as well as other factors (e.g., the outlet of the frontier) obviated the intense economic and ideological struggles which shook Europe. Except during the rapid industrialization of the late nineteenth century and the early years of the twentieth century, during which the Industrial Workers of the World militantly pursued their objectives until routed by the government during World War I, the American worker has played largely an accommodative role and has not challenged the political structure of this country.

Certainly the worker, especially in America, has an unprecedented standard of living.* The relative affluence the worker enjoys cloaks the fact that he or she has a subordinate status and that society does not respect manual labor. Work is more often than not monotonous; it lacks intrinsic value and does not, in most cases, lend itself to upward mobility. The worker has little job security, and his children are more likely than not to inherit his social status.** [45] In the later years of his life he can all too easily fall destitute because of a faulty or insufficient retirement plan. Control over one's work which could make up for the deprivations experienced is virtually nonexistent. This issue is rarely confronted by organized labor. James W. Rinehart has recently pointed out that "unions have managed to improve economic aspects of labor. However they have been unable or unwilling to confront the issue of workers' control over the pace and quality of work, and work standards set by management are reinforced by the unions through its contractual agreement." [46] Alain Touraine referred to a state of confusion among present-day workers in their efforts to fight against their subordinate status.[47] This confusion seems to ensue from a decrescence of plausibility (*Sinn Adequanz*) of traditional working-class symbols (regular employment divests the symbol "unemployment" of its evocative force). The increase of social compensations strips "unemployment" of its political connotations (prospective unemployment is associated with waiting lines for government-subsidized checks,

---

* But so do other classes. Income differentials between social classes persist and have even increased slightly in the last two decades.[44]
** Compared to the bulk of publications in the social sciences, relatively little research has been done on the working class, specifically in the United States. This scarcity of knowledge has no doubt contributed to misconceptions about the working class.

The Maintenance of the Status Quo

not with picket lines demanding the full retention of the labor
force).

Today's working-class symbolism has become so opaque that it
is impossible for the worker to link his situation to an ideological
framework with which he could understand, and more importantly, act upon the deprivation he experiences. After all, socialism,
which contributed most of the working-class symbolism in the
past, suffers from the same problem of plausibility which was
shown to exist for other traditional ideologies. It does not provide
an adequate theoretical and practical interpretation of advanced
industrial society which could serve as a guideline for political
action. This dilemma is aggravated by the linguistic code of the
worker. The concept of alienation, for example, can hardly be
made operative politically because a semantic barrier built of a
restricted language code excludes it from the worker's ideational
world. This sort of difficulty was encountered by West German
trade unions which tried to make the symbol "participation" a
meaningful one for the workers.[48]

In view of the elements of communication analyzed so far, the
obstacles inhibiting political reflection and communication by
members of the lower and working classes are indeed enormous.
Neither linguistic ability nor interpretative schemes permit the
articulation of conflict. What can be seen instead are highly
privatized ways of incorporating conflicts and tensions springing
from the conditions of work and the workers' subordination.
Nonetheless, there is some evidence that this privatization of conflict may not apply to young workers in certain sectors of the
economy, specifically in the automotive industry.* [49]

* There is, particularly among young workers, a growing dissatisfaction due to
the monotony of work and productivity drives conducted at the expense of
the worker. This discontent, as expressed in high employee turn over, ab-
senteeism, careless work, and even acts of sabotage has been placated by some
companies (e.g., Motorola) with some success by reorganizing the production
flow to create more diversified work. In Sweden, the government subsidized
Volvo's attempt to replace completely the classical assembly line in a new
plant. Entire components of cars are put together by groups of workers who
can pace their work rather than operate individually as human adjuncts to
machines.

Supportive Values and Orientations

The workers' acceptance of a subordinate position and their dichotomized view of society as made up of the influential rich on one hand and the hard working poor on the other hardly constitute a false consciousness imposed from above. If the worker were to adhere to the dominant American democratic ideology with its stress on an open society, equality, and political participation, one would not observe the obedience and conformity that are common to large segments of the working and lower classes. Any realization that there are unequal educational and occupational opportunities, that there is inequality before the law and limited social mobility, and that the electoral process does not contribute to change is a realistic but not an ideological appraisal.[50]

The political behavior of the working class is decided not by a concern for civil liberties or a wiser or more equitable use of resources, but by individual members' economic interest in preserving, minimally, a semiaffluent status.[51] Workers' perception of the state as the benefactor whose interventions are welcome if they preserve attained status or insure law and order rather than as what Marx called executive committee for the bourgeoisie obviously serves to perpetuate the workers' subordinate position. Working-class dissatisfaction, wild cat strikes, and the periodic shift of political allegiances from the Democratic Party to one further to the right arise from status anxiety and from the frequently justified conviction that reform programs benefit other groups and are disproportionately financed by the workers' taxes.

A preoccupation with consumerism and leisure, fortified on a daily basis by the media, obscures the worker's awareness of his inferior status at work and in society. A review of the literature suggests that this phenomenon is reported in virtually all industrial societies, even those with a strong working-class tradition. In West Germany, Harriett Moore and Gerhard Kleining found most of the working class resigned to its social position and isolation from other classes.* [52] K. L. Specht noted that salary, job security, and recognition of the work executed are the cardinal values of the German industrial worker.[53] In France the discussion by working-class theoreticians of possible structural changes is subordinated to the concern with the maintenance of the standard of living enjoyed by unionized workers.[54] British studies by John H. Goldthorpe and his associates show that the worker has become politically integrated into the system without, however, accepting the middle-class culture. He concludes that the political behavior of the worker has changed from a "solidaristic collectivism" to an "instrumental orientation" in which the social existence of the workers becomes privatized and "the economic advancement of the individual and his family becomes of greater importance than membership in a closely knit local community." The trade union is seen by workers almost exclusively as a means for improving their standard of living and not as an agency for transforming the social structure.[55] The picture which emerges in the United States is a similar one.

In 1955, Elizabeth L. Lyman found that blue-collar workers in America favored easy work and economic rewards.[56] Three years later Oscar Glantz made the observation that class consciousness was considerably higher among businessmen than among organized workers.[57] In a review of empirical material, Harold Wilensky confirmed Glantz's position in reporting that "the clearest and most consistent awareness of class is at the top." [58] Like Goldthorpe in Britain, James W. Rinehart recently disputed the thesis of embourgeoisement of the worker and stressed the American worker's economic, as distinct from his cultural, integration.[59]

The privatization of conflict and the absence of a range of adequate political symbols have transformed the alleged agent of the revolution into a class that is at least indifferent, if not antagonistic, to social change. Demands which threaten the status quo will hardly come forth from the working class. Receptiveness

---

* A finding that was also applicable to lower echelon white-collar workers.

to governmental authority, constrained communication, and material compensations insure the integration of the working class. And if ideology is a causal factor at all, then it is the absence of a counterideology and not the existence of a pervasive dominant ideology that assures the acceptance of the status quo.

THE STRUCTURE OF DECISION MAKING

Up until now we have seen that the political system is stabilized by the material co-optation of large segments of the population, a process that is amplified by the mass media and continued economic growth, by the justificatory para-ideology of science and technology, and by structural impediments to political communication. Some of these stabilizing factors are, however, only the corollary of the changing role of political institutions. It has been shown that the necessity of economic growth structures political communication. This necessity has also transformed political institutions. Parliamentary politics geared to the mediation of conflicts are slowly being replaced by executive policies oriented toward the effective administration of society. The functional state, to use George Burdeau's term, removes itself from society's problems and conflicts.[60] Accordingly, those political institutions in which conflicts were once articulated can no longer be considered as bodies that carry out political and social change.

The Economics of Decision Making

Most changes in political institutions can be traced to the imperative of maintaining economic growth. The need to institutionalize economic growth requires the centralization of decision-making processes and the extension of governmental power. This increase of power entails a progressive expansion of those domains into which the state can legitimately intervene. The reliance on material and social compensations presupposes that a surplus is generated by the economy. Past interventions by the state into the market were occasional and extraordinary in nature. Current interventions are permanent in character and are determined by the goal of stabilized, predictable economic growth.

The overriding importance of economic growth becomes apparent in the choice of means necessary to attain or to accelerate it. The institutionalization of wage and price controls in 1972 was contrary to Nixon's conservative economics and at least constitutionally questionable because of the retroactive provisions that invalidate existing contracts. But the reorientation of Republican policies becomes comprehensible if the political repercussions of economic stagnation are taken into account. Declining revenues would severely limit the state's expenditures on governmental services as well as its ability to palliate crisis areas. Most importantly, the question of the redistribution of material resources and benefits, suspended in periods of relative affluence, would become politically pregnant during a depression or serious recession when resources are inadequate for the provision of material and social compensations.

The extent of services the state provides in advanced industrial society goes considerably beyond governmental responsibilities in the past. In addition to maintaining an enormous military apparatus and an adequate infrastructure, the state supports, schematically educational, medical, and other institutions; subsidizes corporate farmers and flagging military-oriented corporations; provides welfare, social security, unemployment compensation, manpower training, and so forth; and funds a staggering number of bureaucracies. Today the allocation of state aid is determined, first, by the criterion of potential productivity of the sector to which financial support goes.* Budgetary policies, due to an inflationary or recessive economy, crystallize this priority. Whereas the Ford administration reduced in 1975 outlays for most social welfare programs and for aid to states and localities, it significantly increased the amount of spending in civilian research

---

* To a lesser extent anticipated costs to public agencies are taken into account. If, for example, a problem such as drug addiction has created sufficient financial strain on penal or medical institutions, the state will intervene.

and development projects that were productivity oriented. Because universities and colleges provide the knowledge and skilled manpower necessary for the operation of the components of advanced industrial society, higher education has received substantial funding in the last decade, though compared to European countries this support makes up only a small proportion of total governmental expenditures. Urban decay, on the other hand, as been largely disregarded since it cannot be tied to productivity. Nor have issues such as opportunities for minority groups and the environmental crisis met with consequential political response. Exacerbating official disinterest in an effective solution of these problems is the fact that future commitments of federal revenue seriously curtail the flexibility of national priorities. Because of these commitments, the debate about immanent change in priorities is essentially an exercise in consciousness raising. Expectations of that change being brought about by the replacement of office holders are equally illusionary.

The management of economic development is made possible by several mechanisms. Governmental spending for goods and services has risen more than twentyfold over the last forty years.* This spending insures that in periods of recession consumer demands do not decline too severely. Outlays for the military sector serve as an effective and expedient stimulus for economic growth as well as for scientific and technological research.** [62] Furthermore, they do not add to expectations as expenditures for welfare and antipoverty programs do. In Western Europe, it has become one of the functions of the state to take over, in times of stress, those failing enterprises, the demise of which would threaten overall growth or create an intolerable strain on public services through the costs incurred by widespread unemployment. In the United States a more indirect approach, e.g., government loans to large

---

* It rose from 8.5 billion dollars in 1929 to 212.2 billion dollars in 1969.[61]
** As R. A. Gordon has suggested, "had it not been for the rapid increase in military expenditures and the relative stability of private fixed investments, we [in the United States] should have recorded a true recession in 1967 rather than a 'minirecession'." [63]

industrial enterprises or the creation of semipublic corporations to replace failing ones, serves the same purpose. In advanced capitalist society an evolving corporate socialism comes to the aid of large corporations* and helps insure growth of the G. N. P. thereby securing the system of domination.

Because of the size of the corporations, the interdependence of economic and social institutions, and the consequent mesh between the private and the public sector, an effective organization of the economy requires coherent and consistent economic policies at the national level. The institutionalization of economic growth presupposes long-range planning and the coordination of profit and nonprofit sectors. Long-range planning requires that all factors which could influence the national decision-making process are controlled. This means that the power of decision-making organs other than those charged with planning (i.e., executive and advisory bodies) has to be reduced, particularly that of legislatures.[64]

The Changing Role of Legislative Bodies

The reduction of parliamentary and—to a lesser extent—of judicial power is obviously not an overt, rapid process, but a gradual one. In most cases the shift of power is justified not on substantive grounds, such as the merits of executive power per se, but on financial or administrative grounds. A recent bill proposing the establishment of a national financing bank to administer the distribution of all federally financed credits, which would completely bypass Congress, is a prime example of this trend. The implications of that bill which, according to the New York Times, "was proposed and strongly supported by the Nixon Administration" are far reaching. The executive branch of government would assume direct control over federal and federally assisted credit which amounted in 1971 to 40 per cent of all credit circulating

---

* At the same time there is a growing emphasis on self-help for the unproductive welfare population as seen in recent work requirements for welfare recipients.

that year. The President would have authority to reduce the amount of credit guaranteed by federal institutions. A federal financing bank rather than private banks would be the principal source of credit for federal agencies. It is argued that the country would save up to $300 million a year in interest the government would otherwise pay to private banks and additional sums due to savings in administrative costs were the bill passed into law.[65]

This efficiency would be achieved at the price of enfeebling Congress and aggravating the imbalance of exercised power between the executive and legislative branches of government. A ceiling on federal expenditures as requested by Nixon and passed by the House of Representatives would further eviscerate Congress's power of the purse. The bill was rejected by the Senate in 1972 but reintroduced in the Ninety-third Congress. This spending ceiling would grant to the executive a "retroactive item veto" permitting him to veto funding for existing and proposed programs. It gives to the executive power to eliminate programs initiated by previous administrations, and all indications show that social services would be the first to go. The technocratic rationale of minimizing expenditures and of streamlining administrative power leaves little room for checks and balances, specifically if this control means additional costs and a cumbersome decision-making process. This particular case stands *in nuce* for the development of political decision making in advanced industrial society, namely, the erosion of traditional modes of democratic control. Another means of avoiding parliamentary interference is to request and obtain the power from the legislature to make decisions concerning future policies without specifying the content of these decisions. Such power was granted to Nixon by Congress to combat inflation and unemployment. It goes without saying that there was no consultation with Congress or its leaders about the nature of the regulations to be enacted prior to the announcement of wage and price controls.

The transfer of decision making from Congress, which is in part due to a voluntary abdication on the part of the Congress of its responsibility for policy making, has been most noticeable in foreign affairs, but major social legislation has also been initiated by the White House, for example, the civil rights and antipoverty legislation of the Johnson administration. As has been well established, parliamentary bodies in advanced industrial societies perform increasingly the role of acclamatory institutions.[66] Certainly, legislative measures initiated by Congress are still written into the body of the law, but they appear secondary in importance to those sponsored by the Executive.[67]

The authority of Congress can be measured by the restrictions which are imposed on communication concerning past or prospective executive policies. As mentioned in the discussion of constrained communication, civil servants can refuse to testify before a committee of this body if executive privilege is invoked by the President. Congress can de facto be committed to national policies without prior consultation or consent and can be confronted with actions and decisions which have long-range repercussions for the nation. Executive agreements, which subvert Congressional authority in foreign affairs, have proliferated under the Johnson and Nixon administrations. In 1930 the President concluded nine executive agreements and signed 25 treaties each approved by two-thirds of the Senate. In 1968, 266 executive agreements were concluded and 16 treaties signed into law.[68] By January 1, 1972, "the U.S. was party to a total of 4359 executive agreements and 947 treaties. . . ." [69] Both executive privilege and executive agreements have developed extraconstitutionally.

Representative government is further subverted if the President refuses with impunity to execute laws passed by Congress and condones actions of subordinates that run counter to the spirit and the letter of what is then only technically the law. That the adoption of a law is not tantamount to enforcement is underscored by numerous analysis of the interplay between regulatory agencies and pressure groups.[70] Although regulatory agencies are meant to translate the intent of legislation into viable procedures and regulations, it has become a practice of the White House to intervene actively in operations of these agencies and to redefine Congressional intent. The decision of the Federal Communications Commission to regulate the growth of the cable television industry is one example. In this case the chairman of the commission, as stated in the *New York Times,* had "embraced the changes that the White House made in his earlier proposal. . . . Congressional sources speculated . . . that there would be no interference in a plan that the powerful private interests all accepted." The Justice Department would not intervene since "the new plan already had strong support in other branches of the Nixon administration" even though the plan included provisions, as the *Times* pointed out, which potentially violate antitrust laws.[71]

The loss of authority by Congress entails ipso facto diminishing accountability to the public. It is noteworthy that organizations such as Common Cause and Public Interest rely more and more on the judicial branch of government in the pursuit of their interpretations of the commonweal. Obviously this strategy has its limits because of executive influence over appointments to the federal bench.

Parallel to the reduction of parliamentary participation in the decision-making process is the loss of power by local and state authorities in matters bearing directly or indirectly on the economy. The rationalization of the decision-making process, introduced to stabilize the status quo by making economic development as predictable as possible, becomes ineffective if state and local authorities have the power to alter plans or to stall their execution. There is also both a voluntary and a forced abdication by state and local governments of responsibility in the social sector. In part this abdication is due to the absence of a viable revenue sharing plan and the limits of the tax base of states and local communities, which makes it difficult to meet the costs of programs that are often determined by federal legislation. With the glaring acceleration of urban decay, governors and mayors expect that the federal government accept a large part of the financial burden for social programs. Clearly, these problems of the infra-structure can no longer be resolved on the local or state level. A national response will, however, further erode the autonomy of state and municipal government.

Apart from the necessity to centralize economic and societal development, there are several secondary factors which contribute to the shift in decision making. Congressional inertia regarding its declining power in combination with a presidential system accelerates the concentration of power. This process is not checked by American political parties which lack the organizational and popular bases of European parties.[72] American political parties have, by and large, remained parties of notables with a regional instead of a national character. Temporary coalitions against presidential power are unstable. The idea that a public interest exists above and beyond particularistic interests is hardly well developed. The public welfare is defined in praxis as the sum total of private interests, which means that the most articulate and best financed groups define it. Economic pressure groups obviously support any policy oriented toward the institutionalization of economic growth. And they do not oppose those structural changes in political institutions that such a policy may imply. It is the above changes in political institutions that have forestalled changes in the system of domination.

By gaining control over institutions which are beyond the traditional domain of the government, the state has become pivotal in the management of advanced industrial society. Considering the directive power of the executive, it appears unlikely that structural changes can be brought about through parliamentary institutions since they seem to have exhausted their functions in advanced industrial society. As General de Gaulle stated, in modern times politics has become too important to be left to the politicians.

The attempts to control and administer society may create conflict zones that cannot be contained with higher wages, more leisure time, and the promise of affluence. The productivity of advanced industrial society permits the extensive use of these compensations; whether or not they suffice to legitimate the political order and to ensure the normative compliance of groups other than the working class is an open question which will be analyzed in the following chapter.

4

THE CRISIS OF GOVERNMENTAL AUTHORITY

Journalistic and literary writing about contemporary society draws from the imagery of 1984 and the *Brave New World* to describe the tentacular reach of government, an imagery which is suggestive indeed insofar as the rise of an overarching state is concerned. The role of government is so pervasive in advanced industrial society that no institutional sector is left untouched by it. Social, economic, and cultural institutions as well as individuals have become dependent on political institutions for development and survival.

This accretion of governmental influence is compounded by the complexity of advanced industrial society which interlocks all institutional areas and requires a coordination of all units of the social system.* As distinct from past political systems, not excluding seventeenth century absolutism, advanced industrial society require citizens to submit to the consequences of a myriad of decisions over which they have little if any control. This submission would be no problem if coercion were effective or if man

---

* Institutions are, in the sociological sense, distinguished by their respective functions in and for society and by different types of social interaction and norms that are unique to them. The term is used here in that sense when referring to the institution of politics, economy, education, the family, etc.

could be thoroughly conditioned to a prescribed point of view; but man is not fashioned in toto according to the needs of a social system. He is an unfinished social and political product who adds his own impressions to society's imprint. Because the government and secondary socialization agencies have a limited formative influence on a personality, contradictions can arise between the perception of the individual and the image the political system presents of itself, between his expectations and the systems performance.

Any government, particularly in democratic societies, operates on the trust which the governed credit it and its agencies. If citizens perceive of institutions, procedures, and ruling groups as legitimate, tensions and instability arising from the gap between official and individual interpretations can be absorbed. Scarcity, deprivation, and frustrated aspirations can be endured if the reasons to do so are convincing enough. No matter how critical or conformable an individual may be, whether his language code is restricted or elaborated, a belief in the legitimacy of a political system will considerably augment his willingness to tolerate shortcomings of the political order.

The expansion of the government into institutional areas and everyday life and the resultant direct or indirect management of the population makes a political system more vulnerable. It assumes at least the passive collaboration of the public. Any extension of rule into areas traditionally alien to politics requires plausible legitimating rationales without which such rule would meet resistance. The strengths or weaknesses of legitimating beliefs act upon the stability or instability of a political system. An analysis of society's legitimating principles is similar to a surgical probing for that which is unseen, but nevertheless crucial for survival. A number of theoretical analyses of legitimacy will be reviewed as a prelude to the following evaluation of current claims to legitimacy. These claims will than be considered in relation to those conditions which make for conflict and to the political orientations of the middle classes.

LEGITIMACY IN MODERN SOCIETY

Legitimacy as the Basis of Domination and Authority

Domination, to recapitulate, designates the control of a limited number of individuals over the material resources of society and over the access to positions of political power. Legitimacy confers authority on a system of domination, making its decisions regarding policies, priorities, or the allocation of resources rightful. Legitimating rationales, necessary to any system of domination, are effective only if their underlying principles have been internalized by the public, that is, collectively accepted as normative and thus as binding.

Legitimacy, once established, serves as the most effective justification for the manner in which political power is exercised. It is the most effective argument against attempts to change the structure of the political system.* On the other hand, challenges to governmental systems that question their legitimacy are the most damaging. During the demise of monarchies, advocates of democracy could convincingly evoke the principles of a social contract or the people's sovereignty as bases for legitimacy in opposition to monarchic principles of dynastic lineage and divine right.

There is no political system in which power or the ability to exert influence on the decision-making process is distributed equally among members of the political community. Within the

---

* Prior to the French Revolution, Louis XVI made, in opposition to the convocation of a representative assembly, the following declaration which affirmed the undivisible power of the king: "Those principles, which are universally accepted by the nation, stipulate that to the King alone belongs the sovereign power in his kingdom; that this exercise of power is accountable only to God; that the link which unites the King and the nation cannot by its nature be dissolved; that the mutual obligations of the King and his subjects can only ensure the perpetuation of this union; that the nation has an interest in making sure that the rights of its commander are not changed whatsoever; that the King is the supreme commander of the nation and is one with the nation; [and] finally, that the power to make laws resides in the person of the Sovereign without dependence or division." [1]

limits of constitutional or procedural boundaries, governments respond primarily to the most powerful interests and distribute available resources accordingly. This obviously means that societal needs are satisfied unequally. By obfuscating the link between a system of domination and the class- or group-specific interests this system serves, any legitimating rationale has an ideological foundation. This ideological element becomes apparent if justifications for domination, such as historical materialism, majority rule, divine right, and the alleged superiority of a race, are examined. Ideologies, and the justifications embedded in them, demonstrate their utility, as Jürgen Habermas argues, in their capacity to stabilize political systems which always require some form of legitimation.[2]

David Easton, writing from a different theoretical perspective, sees a similar function in the popular belief in a system's legitimacy. As he suggests "under most conditions, it [this belief] represents a requirement, which, if it is not fulfilled, may find a system unable to marshal enough support or general political will for its persistence in any form. . . . *Nor is there any more secure way to regulate the cleavages that appear in all systems so that they do not irreparably rend asunder the fabric of political life*" [emphasis added].[3]

The popularly acknowledged legitimacy of a governmental system permits the successful forwarding of the claim that governmental decisions are normative and therefore obligatory. Legitimating beliefs provide the necessary inducement to accept domination as manifested in governmental rule. Max Weber, who initiated the examination of legitimacy among social scientists in the 1890's, wrote that the behavior of the ruled, where authority is accepted as legitimate, is influenced in such a way that they obey commands as if they were self-evident, natural, and identical with their own convictions.[4] As distinct from coercion, authority has the peculiar attribute of meeting little or no resistance in its exercise. Since legitimacy induces voluntary submission to domination, all political systems will try to instill the belief that their domination is legitimate, whatever the source of this legitimacy may be. Democratic societies have institutionalized civic education in order to perpetuate the belief in democratic legitimacy. Absolutist monarchies have persecuted those espousing liberal views. Napoleon Bonaparte held plebiscites to appeal to the nascent belief in democracy. But he also exploited the monarchistic tradition of legitimacy by making himself emperor[5] and by marrying the daughter of an emperor whose legitimacy and the legitimacy of whose throne was unquestioned, thereby hoping to authenticate the dynastic prerogatives he had arrogated.

The greater success dominant groups have in nurturing and reinforcing belief in the legitimacy of a system, the less resistance they will face in the exercise of their power. Easton emphasized this point by stating, "the inculcation of a sense of legitimacy [is] probably the most effective device for regulating the flow of diffuse support in favor of the authorities and of the regime. . . . The most stable support will derive from the conviction on the part of the member that it is right and proper for him to accept and obey the authorities and to abide by the requirements of the regime." [6]

Certainly, a congruence between the citizen's perception of what is right and proper and the actual performance of the government buttresses a system's claim to legitimacy. But what is important is that the belief in legitimacy results in voluntary submission to political domination even if particular policies are contrary to the interests of the citizens. A government, if considered legitimate, can decide to go to war or increase personal taxation in the face of opposition without threatening the stability of the system. Legitimacy permits a relatively stable margin of operation as well as of error.

Hannah Arendt, unlike Habermas who has argued that a legitimating ideology is a functional prerequisite for a political system's stability, does not perceive of all legitimating principles as ideological in character and has proposed that the decline of authority in Western society is due to the disconnection of authority from moral principles.[7] A similar position is argued by John H. Schaar. Reviewing contemporary definitions of legitimacy, he wrote that the traditional concept of legitimacy based on "custom, divine law, the law of nature, [or] a constitution . . . has been trimmed of its cumbersome 'normative' and 'philosophical' parts."[8] The belief in legitimacy has become a function of the system's ability to manipulate public opinion. For Schaar, the suspension of higher principles as legitimating rationales undercuts the foundations of authority. These two views follow from the premise that neither the actual exercise of authority nor the popular belief in a system's legitimacy are in themselves a sufficient basis for legitimacy. In order for legitimating beliefs to be normatively binding, there has to have been a norm prior to the norm in operation, an indisputable external source of legitimacy, be it a moral principle, a religious precept, a philosophical tenet, or an ideology which is independent of any particular system of government.*

According to the views of Arendt, Habermas, and Schaar, legitimacy cannot viably be reduced to a product of the political system as a consensus can be. The existence of a political system over a long period of time can contribute to that system's acceptance by the population, and continued efficiency of its operation can induce compliance.[10] But neither habituation nor efficiency creates voluntary submission to authority to the extent that a higher principle does. In a democratic society higher principles are self-

---

* The relation between authority and higher principles is clearly demonstrated in Hannah Arendt's analysis of politics. She writes, "the Preamble to the Declaration of Independence would provide the sole source of authority from which the Constitution, not as an act of constituting government but as the law of the land, derives its own legitimacy; for the Constitution itself, in its preamble as well as in its amendments which form the Bill of Rights, is singularly silent on this question of ultimate authority. The authority of self-evident truth may be less powerful than the authority of an 'avenging God,' but it certainly still bears clear signs of divine origin; such truths are, as Jefferson wrote in the original draft of the Declaration of Independence, 'sacred and undeniable'."[9]

evident theologic truths,* government by the governed, self-determination, governmental accountability to the people, and a variety
of social goals that may or may not be explicitly stated in a constitution. Ideally, the right and title to rule would be justified not
simply by adherence to legal procedures, but by principles these
procedures are meant to express, which may be codified in a constitution and are formally beyond dispute. In fact, reference to
ultimate principles has receded in most contemporary discussions
of legitimacy. These discussions focus on the role the state plays
in the sustenance and creation of legitimacy without considering
the function of communication in that process. Constrained,
rather than open, political communication is required for a system
where legitimacy emanates neither from higher principles nor
from the belief of the population, but is produced, like another
candidate, missile, or foreign policy, by the political system itself.

Weber's discussion of the place of legitimacy in industrial society will be briefly summarized because it was the first, and is still
an influential, analysis that has disconnected legitimating rationales
from moral principles to embed them as much in the legal framework of society as in the beliefs of the citizen. For Weber, each
political system justifies itself by appealing to its legitimating principles.[12] In order for this appeal to be successful, the content of
the appeal must correspond to the values, interest, and motivations** of the members of a political community. According to
Weber, "genuine legitimate rule" requires at least a minimum of
voluntary compliance. Since his theoretical approach takes as a
point of departure the individual, the behavior and conceptions
of the social actor are decisive in Weber's notion of legitimacy and
obedience. He accords greater weight to the variables of social

---

* "We hold these truths to be self-evident, that all men are created equal, that
they are *endowed by their Creator* with certain unalienable Rights, that among
these are Life, Liberty and the pursuit of Happiness. That to secure these
rights, Governments are instituted among Men, deriving their just power from
the consent of the governed" [Emphasis added].[11]
** The term motivation refers to distinct values, goals, and psychic states that
activate and direct individual behavior.

interdependence and interaction than to a presumed paramount social system engulfing all of society and all human action. Legitimacy is ascribed to the social order by the citizen instead of being produced by the political system itself; a political order is valid only insofar as validity is bestowed on it by the individual.[13]

The reasons for compliance can range from "simple habituation to the most purely rational calculation of advantage." [14] Weber considers foundations of domination to be unstable if the citizenry accepts it for reasons of personal gain, habit, or emotional attachment. Political domination is stable only if it is based on legitimating principles, principles which he describes as traditional, charismatic, or legal-rational. Weber proposed that in modern Western society legitimacy has been founded on the belief in legality, adding that ethical or esthetic values could possibly sustain the legitimacy of an order as well. Where the legal-rational principle obtains, legitimacy has been bestowed by the citizen because enacted policies are executed according to formally constituted laws and procedures. Laws and procedures "may be treated as legitimate because [they] derive from a voluntary agreement of the interested parties [or are] imposed by an authority which is held to be legitimate and therefore meets with compliance." [15]

Legal-rational legitimacy is translated into a form of authority which rests on impersonal, legally constituted rules. The exercise of authority is not vested in individuals but in offices. As distinct from the traditional or charismatic ruler, the modern ruler functions within the limits of the authority of his office. The right to make decisions and the purview of these decisions is carefully delimited by laws and procedures. Compliance is given to a norm rather than a person and the right to dominate, to exercise authority, is legitimated by constituted rules. Compliance rests on a "belief in the legality of enacted rules and the right of those elevated to authority under such rules to issue commands." [16] Weber proposed that the principle of legal-rational domination found its foremost expression in bureaucratic domination.[17]

There are several points worth noting in Weber's analysis of legitimacy. From a Weberian perspective, practically all political orders experience the need to validate themselves.* They acquire validity, however, only to the degree that the action of their members is "guided by the belief in the existence of a legitimate order." ** [19] In the absence of such belief, other factors may induce acquiescence to political rule, but they can also foment instability. The Weberian conception of legal-rational legitimacy stands midway between classical and modern theories of legitimacy.

Modern notions of legitimacy, as they are held by dominant groups, could be described as salesmanship of the inevitable. In advanced industrial society, legal-rational legitimation is replaced by a technocratic legitimation which does not accord any significance to the beliefs of the citizen or to morality per se. This legitimation grants to political institutions an autonomy and detachment from the public that seems to be as indisputable as the moral principles of traditional legitimacies. Deprived of moral and consensual referents, technocratic legitimation is completely "secularized" and establishes legitimacy either (1) through the manipulation of public opinion or (2) through the provision of material compensations. Seymour M. Lipset describes the first type of modern legitimation when he defines legitimacy as the "capacity of the system to engender and maintain the belief that the existing political institutions are the most appropriate ones for the society." [21] The idea of co-optation is implicit in the second type of modern legitimation. Carl J. Friedrich refers to the present-day belief that "the ruler who improves the standard of living will be considered legitimate." [22]

The para-ideology of science and technology discussed in the

* Exceptions are political orders where the interests of the ruler and his subordinates are identical and the subjects are powerless. In such a case there is not even the pretense of claiming legitimacy.[18]
** David Easton comes close to Weber's position that, in the ultimate analysis, the subjective interpretation of the members of society determines the stability of a political system. "Regardless of how members may be led to perceive the flow of output stimuli and even if they do not see any outputs at all, they alone are able to measure their actual experiences of life against culturally developed expectations of what is desirable and possible." [20]

previous chapter provides the background assumptions for technocratic legitimation. It suggests that the political system is autonomous and capable of solving all social and political problems by drawing upon scientific and technological developments. Institutional interdependence and the pre-eminence of the political sector noted above seem to have made effective conditioning of society possible as is implied by technocratic legitimation. Some social scientists believe this to be not only possible, but insist that such guidance by governmental institutions is a functional prerequisite for the maintenance of complex political systems. A correspondence between policies and either legality or any ultimate principle is secondary. What counts instead is the passive acceptance by the population of all policies.

There is probably no better argument for the technocratic rationale as the basis for legitimacy than that suggested by the German sociologist and administrative expert, Niklas Luhmann. His theory is important for a number of reasons. Luhmann's conception of legitimacy is one of the few coherently argued theoretical justifications of the demise of democratic institutions. It represents an attempt to provide both a legitimating rationale for present-day domination as well as formulas for coping with conflicts, and it carries to the extreme what a number of influential American social scientists, like Karl W. Deutsch, Seymour M. Lipset, Richard M. Merelman, Herman Kahn, and in a more limited sense, David Easton and Talcott Parsons, have been arguing. His theory is an example par excellence of the technocratic reasoning which pervades political institutions in advanced industrial society. Since traditional legitimating principles are exhausted, so to speak,* the technocratic legitimation is the only remaining justificatory rationale for domination in advanced industrial society. An analysis of this rationale should shed some

---

* Cf. John H. Schaar's comment: "Democracy is the most prostituted word of our age, and any man who employs it in reference to any modern state should be suspect either of ignorance or of bad motives." [23]

light both on its plausibility and the viability of the type of system it supports.

Luhmann advances the proposition that the complexity of the social system and the pace of change in advanced industrial society require a decision-making process which can respond immediately to issues and conflicts. He argues that the very existence of advanced industrial society would be threatened if the political system were to attempt to legitimate itself through traditional democratic modes of legitimation. Given the complexity of advanced industrial society and of the conflicts which have to be resolved, the traditional means of arriving at a consensus regarding political questions have become obsolete and have been replaced by procedures. "Procedures" themselves, that is, "generalized, indirect mechanisms which permit the establishment of meaning and stability," * have become the legitimating principle and any return to traditional rationales would be neither feasible nor practical. Luhmann also refers to procedures as "a social system of a particular nature," but nowhere does he give a precise definition of the term.[24] It can be said that he conceives of procedures as being the most efficient modes of action to structure the decision-making process. Procedures are understood to be relatively autonomous. Their purpose is to insure the possibility of formulating binding decisions. According to Luhmann, this new means of legitimating a system of domination can be provided only by the political system itself.

If the social system** of a society is highly complex, the legitimation of political power can no longer be left to a presupposed morality. . . . A power is . . . legitimate which admits and even institutionalizes its own process of legitimation. In addition it must be guaranteed that

---

* In Weber's understanding, procedures are legally constituted. For Luhmann, a procedure may or may not have a legal basis.
** Luhmann uses the term "social system" to denote (a) the sum total of all social interactions in a society, (b) interactions which take place in institutional areas which are sometimes referred to as subsystems, e.g., the political system or subsystem, (c) procedures, and even (d) personalities.

obligatory decisions are accepted as a premise of behavior without prior specification of the decision.[25]

A major and perpetual goal of political institutions, according to Luhmann, is to reduce complexity. This reduction is made possible by eliminating from the decision-making process all elements which complicate it. He therefore repudiates the idea that conceptions of good or evil, truth, and justice should enter decision making. Complexity is also reduced by the separation of the social system from political institutions and the regulation of the different units of the social system. Efficiency in decision making requires that decisions be disconnected from collective values and motivations of the members of a political community, because these values, if taken into account, would narrow the range of possible decisions. Decisions must be freed from any serious consideration of the political or social values of the population. It is Luhmann's contention that competent decisions could not be made if open communication were tolerated because contradictory and competing opinions would needlessly increase the complexity of the decision-making process, and, therefore, it must be avoided. Administrative procedures are meant to reduce the number of opinions the decision makers have to take into account.[26]

Procedures utilized in arriving at a decision, and not the reasons or principles underlying a decision, make a decision acceptable to the population. Luhmann completely separates the legitimacy of a decision from its factual or moral content. He defines legitimacy as the population's "willingness to accept, within certain limits of toleration, decisions which are as yet undetermined in their nature." He does not specify these "limits of toleration." Acceptance of decisions becomes the norm, and the citizens are expected to comply with them "as a premise of their own behavior and to restructure their expectations accordingly." [27] This adjustment of expectations is similar to the learning process, which, in the ideal case leads to the automatic adoption of expectations as dictated by political decisions. Luhmann holds that submission to decisions should be disconnected from personal convictions and that it should result from the fact that the validity of the official decision is taken for granted.

The legitimation of decisions involves basically an effective learning process in the social system, a process which should be free from disturbances. It is part of the general problem of "how expectations change," of the question as to how the political-administrative sub-system of society can restructure the expectations of society through decisions even though it itself is only a sub-system. The effectiveness of such an activity of one segment of the whole depends on its ability to build new expectations into other existing systems—whether they are personalities or social systems.[28]

The restructuring of expectations transforms governmental bureaucracies into managing agents charged with directing instructional processes that narrow the range of alternatives, disconnect law and politics from other social mechanisms, and condition the population to whatever the survival of the system requires.[29] The actual political decision-making process is disconnected from other social processes as well because the latter give rise to beliefs and values which embody traditional views that do not sufficiently take the complexity of modern society into account.

To date, the instruction the political system is meant to provide has not been administered effectively. Compliance to authority may be due to traditional or "unrealistic" values and cannot be taken for granted. The complexity of the social system becomes greater each day and generates the potential for instability and societal conflicts. Anything less than total compliance becomes an obstacle which governmental institutions have to continually surmount. The traditional instruments of governmental rule, such as electoral and judicial mechanisms, absorb these conflicts while preventing them from interfering in any substantive way with the political system. These conflicts are refracted or, as Luhmann puts it, transformed in order that "they become politicized in a harmless way." [30]

The transformation of conflicts into nonissues is made possible by the role electoral institutions play in modern society. Elections, says Luhmann, cannot provide solutions to societal conflicts nor do they serve to express concrete interests. They have, for the most, an integrative function in that they perpetuate the public's illusion of participation in politics. Rather than deciding policies, elections "neutralize, or at least splinter, the influence societal structures have on the political system." Luhmann approves the declining power of the legislative branch of government by arguing that only specialized bodies are able to deal with complex subject matters. The demise of parliamentary institutions is functional for the maintenance of a political system as are a population's "ignorance and apathy" which Luhmann believes to be "the most important preconditions for the generally unnoticed change of legal arrangements." [31]

Social mobility, nondistorted communication, and the ability to perceive alternatives create tensions in the political system. These tensions are aggravated by the increasing complexity and the confluent individualization of personalities. These threats to system stability are counteracted by effectively propagating trust in the political system and removing the latter from the center of public debate. Luhmann postulates that the political manipulation of all grievances becomes crucial for the stability of the social order and that "the mechanisms which regulate and diffuse dissatisfaction . . . have to become much more efficient." [32]

Luhmann concludes his analysis by stressing that the behavior of the individual must be made to be predictable and to conform to the demands of advanced industrial society. The task of removing the dysfunctional individual or class-specific motivations from the political realm is supposed to be performed by "mechanisms of mutual indifference" which are placed between the personal and social system.[33]

Essentially, Luhmann's position on legitimacy means that the population unreservedly submits itself to a "restructuring of expectations" as stipulated by directives of the political system.

From his perspective, order cannot be maintained by coercion or voluntary submission in the name of some higher principle, but by the administrative adjustment of personality structures and social systems to the political-administrative apparatus. This means that governments must continually adapt the population and institutions to whatever they believe to be necessary for the maintenance of the social order. Society's complexity and public enlightenment are mutually exclusive. Learning processes are restricted to the acquisition of norms and values which conform to the requirements of stability and other demands of the political order. The solution of political and social problems is left to experts who are allegedly able to cope with complexity. Political authority has a strictly functional character since the goal of preserving the economic system, rather than the goal of representing the populace, defines its policies.

Several theoretical fallacies in Luhmann's theory are evident, particularly in light of the material reviewed in previous chapters, to say nothing of the philosophical values he projects or reflects. The assumption that political behavior can be disconnected from collective values is contrary to evidence garnered from research on the political socialization process. The belief that procedures alone suffice to maintain legitimacy cannot be reconciled with the need for a legitimating ideology experienced by past and present societies. Most studies of advanced industrial society negate Luhmann's hypothesis that the exercise of political power is independent of class-specific interests. The proposition that a synchronization of the social and the political system could be achieved, though perhaps theoretically and politically attractive to conservatives, is, however, dubious in view of the conflicts advanced industrial societies actually experience.

These fallacies are, however, secondary in importance in comparison with the ideological character of Luhmann's theory of legitimacy. Luhmann affirms and justifies the existing system of domination by dismissing the relevance of all interests except that of system maintenance. He does not admit to the existence of

142 · The Politics of Communication

political domination.[34] Luhmann's version of the technocratic legitimation becomes potent if combined with an additional legitimating rationale, namely, efficiency.

If the ruled and the ruler's interpretations of political reality are no longer guided by moral principles and if legal-rational rule is transformed into technocratic management of society, the acceptance of a political system is determined by considerations of efficiency. Efficiency as a source of legitimacy is implied, but not explicit, in Luhmann's theory. This source of legitimacy can be understood as the belief of the population that the political system is capable of providing promised services and of satisfying existing and anticipated needs. Certainly, the principle of efficiency as a source of legitimacy is not new. Historically, leaders had to meet certain expectations arising from the past and would undermine the legitimacy of their rule if they proved incapable of giving to the population what tradition prescribed. Elements of efficiency enter into the impression management of the successful charismatic leader. Legal-rational domination is also akin to efficiency since impersonal norms and rules allow for predictability, ergo, efficient administration. Efficiency, although necessary to all three modes of domination, is not, however, the decisive component.

Weber placed great emphasis on the processes of rationalization and bureaucratization without which the effectiveness of a political system could not be maintained. The scarcity of the nineteenth and early twentieth century combined with perpetual economic instability precluded the political use of material compensations as a basis for the continued loyalty of the mass of the population. Efficiency was seen, not as a source of legitimacy, but as an organizing principle permitting the development of the forces of production and of rational administration.*

* In 1917 Weber argued that "the 'progress' toward the bureaucratic state, adjudicating and administering according to rationally established law and regulation, is nowadays very closely related to modern capitalist development. The modern capitalist enterprise rests primarily on *calculation* and presupposes

Today, efficiency is an important, if not the most important, source of legitimacy in modern society. The disconnection of politics from a normative basis and the decline of traditional legitimating ideologies and collectively held political interpretations, on one hand, and the growing intervention of the state into the social and economic order, on the other, have created a symbolic void which has to be filled by legitimating symbols of a new nature. As noted before, the para-ideology of science and technology fills some of the vacuum by defining the framework within which political decisions are made. A more concrete justification for political domination is the prospect of ever-climbing affluence, of efficiency as demonstrated in the delivery of goods to consume, services to please, and time to enjoy it all.

In contemporary discussions of domination, efficiency is viewed as a legitimating as well as an organizing principle. Friedrich, for instance, proposed a new form of legitimacy for modern society, namely, a "procedural and pragmatic" legitimacy. The procedural aspect is the electoral mechanism; the pragmatic is a society's "performance preferences . . . such as success in war, prosperity, . . . order and peace. . . . Democratic legitimacy in modern states is . . . subject to performance tests, especially in the economic realm." [36] The individual's belief in the legitimacy of the political system is thus determined by the actual performance of the system. This is implied by Lipset when he states that the stability of modern society hinges on economic development and on effectiveness. He defines effectiveness as "actual performance, the extent to which the system satisfies the basic functions of government as most of the population and such powerful groups within it as big business and the armed forces see them." [37]

The citizen would presumably consider domination legitimate if the expectation of efficiency is met. From the technocratic view-

a legal and administrative system whose functioning can be rationally predicted, at least in principle, by virtue of its fixed general norms, just like the expected performance of a machine." [35]

point, legitimacy based on efficiency could be sustained through the control or restructuring of expectations when the system fails to operate efficiently. But the individual's perception of society and legitimacy is not necessarily identical with that of the technocrat. Expectations are not uniform. After all, what motivates the population politically is bound up with everyday experiences and events that are shaped by the class structure. Any response to claims to legitimacy is likely to be group-specific.

The pragmatic orientation of the working class accords priority to material benefits. This orientation responds more readily to a claim to legitimacy founded on efficiency than to a claim which stresses the legal-rational basis for decision making. Specifically in the United States, large segments of the population are more concerned with efficiency, with whether or not given policies serve their material interests, than with issues focusing on legality, moral principles, or societal goals. A concern for legitimacy as it springs from legal-rational procedures for candid public debate and for democratic principles such as effective participation in the decision-making process, tends to set apart affluent segments of the population where nonconforming world views have been encouraged since childhood. Support or withdrawal of support from the political system is conditioned by factors specific to each social class or group. Nonetheless, no matter which legitimating rationale is presented to different classes, it must be sustained politically and socially.

The Sustenance of Legitimacy

There is one point of agreement among the classical and modern writers discussed so far which is that each political system must continually sustain its legitimacy. This sustenance of legitimacy is, however, more problematic than it would appear at first glance. Talcott Parsons has suggested that an institutional arrangement of society can be maintained if the social system can provide the population with adequate material and cultural resources. The fulfilment of needs is a requisite for system stability, but what is just as important for the support of the political order is the subjective commitment of the population that is instilled by a society's cultural institutions.* [38]

. One could argue that legitimacy can be successfully sustained if (1) material needs can be met, (2) the political system can decisively influence public communication, (3) support from the cultural strata is available, and (4) supportive values of the population at large can be regenerated. The material needs of politically relevant groups have to be fulfilled, that is, the needs of those groups whose cooperation in the economic process is an absolute necessity. The institutionalization of economic growth in advanced capitalism would seem to create enough surplus to meet these needs.

In order to control communication, the political system must engage in effective impression management. It has to present itself to the public as the best possible system in order to prevent other institutional arrangements from being considered by the public as meaningful alternatives. This impression management is carried out through the mechanisms of constrained communication discussed in the previous chapter. The government can successfully contain public discussion by withholding information, misleading the public about its intentions, or suppressing evidence that sheds an unfavorable light on its policies or that reveals truths about a society that would profoundly disrupt it.

* Parsons writes that "a social system cannot be so structured as to be radically incompatible with the conditions of functioning of its component individual actors as biological organisms and as personalities, or of the relatively stable integration of a cultural system. . . . In turn the social system, on both fronts, depends on the requisite minimum of 'support' from each of the other systems. It must, that is, have a sufficient proportion of its component actors adequately motivated to act in accordance with the requirements of its role system, positively in the fulfillment of expectations and negatively in abstention from too much disruptive, i.e., deviant, behavior. . . . The obverse of the functional prerequisite of meeting a minimum proportion of the needs of the individual actors, is the need to secure adequate participation of a sufficient proportion of these actors in the social system, that is, to motivate them adequately to the performances which may be necessary if the social system in question is to persist or develop." [39]

But as the cases of Daniel Ellsberg and of journalists who refuse to collaborate with grand jury proceedings demonstrate, control over communication cannot be securely maintained in a non-
totalitarian system if members of the *cultural strata* do not
cooperate. Those whose work is devoted to the analysis of society
and the elaboration of symbolic representations of society, those
who are moved to reflect upon the nature of man and his world
or simply to act on the moral impulse that *Realpolitik* does not
admit to, cannot be contained or commodified. The cultural and
normative foundation of society is born by writers, poets, journalists, social scientists, educators, publishers, civically involved law-
yers, doctors, scientists, and religious leaders as well as by film
makers, painters, and all other artists. They inspire and sustain
reflection in others. Because their work is not dependent upon
dominant economic and political interests, persons belonging to
this cultural stratum can function in ways which immure themselves, in comparison to other occupational groups, from official
interpretations of reality. The professions of most of these people
require that they are well informed and educated, ergo numerous
studies and simple observation attest to the cultural and educational status that define this stratum as a group. Members of this
group share knowledge of the political process and the ability to
cope with and manipulate symbols. Traditionally, groups such as
this one mediated the legitimacy of a political system by either
transmitting through their work the belief that the political system
was proper and warranted loyalty or by formulating alternatives.
In contemporary society it is that segment of the population which
is most politicized.

As studies of social change demonstrate, the political positions
the cultural stratum take are crucial for the stability and the
sustenance of legitimacy of the political system. This stratum's
contribution, specifically of intellectuals, to stability or instability
has been observed both by classical and modern social scientists.
For Marx and Weber, whose theoretical perspectives were far
apart, intellectuals serve to preserve or revise the images society

has of itself. According to Marx's view, the participation of intellectuals is necessary for the development of a revolutionary consciousness among the working class. Weber, pointing to the material and ideal interests that govern man's conduct, held that "very frequently the 'world images' that have been created by 'ideas' have, like switchmen, determined the tracks along which action has been pushed by the dynamic of interest." [40] Specifically in his early writings he emphasized that the work of intellectuals (as reflected in ideas or belief systems) played an important role in social development and the evolution of history itself.

In contemporary analysis, growing emphasis is placed on the cultural strata. Suzanne Keller, among others, discusses political, cultural, and economic "elites" and suggests that these groups play a more important role in modern society than in past societies and that their beliefs and values are more essential for the survival of society than those of the rest of the population. "Today," she writes, "the collective conscience may be considered to be the conscience of the men in strategic elite positions. . . . The strategic elites of complex societies are a link between past and future, a bridge to the moral survival of all." [41] It follows that in her analysis, popular consensus regarding political goals is secondary. Instead "effective social life [requires] moral accord among strategic elites. . . . As societies become more differentiated a considerable degree of consensus is needed at the top. . . . The absence of moral consensus is often held accountable for severe problems besetting modern nations." [42] The historian Crane Brinton suggests in his comparative study of revolutions that "the transfer of allegiance of the intellectuals . . . is in some respects the most reliable of the symptoms" of a revolutionary situation.[43]

Given the scarcity of empirical material, it is difficult to enumerate with certainty those factors which encourage or corrode the support of political institutions by the cultural strata. The least one can say is that socioeconomic stability and a relative correspondence between generally accepted ideals and actual conditions are conducive to support, whereas the absence of these factors contributes to the potential for discontent and opposition. To be certain, these groups, even if unified, could not induce structural change. But such change presupposes among other factors an ideological framework which intellectuals provide.

Support from the cultural strata is also one element which contributes to the fourth condition for the sustenance of legitimacy; the regeneration of values necessary for the maintenance of political and economic institutions. Because legitimacy has to be reinforced among all citizens, even in periods of stability, the values which uphold a system must become the personal values of those living in it. It is obvious that a society which finds its legitimating rationales in material welfare has to perpetuate, with Sisyphean zeal, consumerism in all the guises that its industries and their advertising agencies can contrive. Successful regeneration of supportive values assumes that the primary and secondary socialization processes are synchronized and that *cognitive dissonance*, that is, discrepancies between the individual's acquired values and his experience in society, can be reduced or at least regulated. The analysis of class-specific socialization strategies and educational institutions in Chapter 2 revealed that, by and large, supportive values are transmitted in lower-class families and school systems, whereas middle-class families, schools, and certain disciplines in higher education impart values and orientations which are antithetical to those upon which the political system is founded. The synchronization of secondary and primary socialization is therefore only successful in the lower classes.

Cognitive dissonance and resulting dissatisfaction could be diffused in the past through the successful propagation of an ideology which made acceptable the temporary or permanent repression of unfulfilled needs and expectations. Because there is no longer a dominant ideology compelling enough to prompt people to relinquish either quantitative or qualitative needs, that strategy of deflection has lost its effect. The absence of an ideology and structural changes in advanced industrial society, which obviously do not leave the individual's political views untouched, have created and are creating conflicts that cannot be resolved solely with coercion, manipulation, or co-optation.

SOCIAL AND POLITICAL
CONDITIONS FOR CONFLICT

The theory that the decline of powerful nations is inevitable because each political order carries the seeds of its own demise was propounded in the early part of this century by Oswald Spengler. Before Spengler, Marx proposed that the liberating power of the forces of production would ultimately destroy the capitalist system. Joseph Schumpeter, writing in the early forties, proposed that neither a sudden economic crisis nor class struggle would lead to the downfall of capitalism. Instead, the rise of corporate bureaucracies would mark the disappearance of the capitalist entrepreneur and destroy the function of the bourgeoisie as a class. In recent social theory these interpretations have been put aside as unwarranted prophecies of doom. Dysfunctions of the system have been regarded as temporary aberrations which can be taken care of.

The social and political turmoil of the sixties in Western Europe and the United States which appeared to be at odds with orderly economic and social development as envisaged by theoreticians, has required rethinking in order to adjust theory to reality. The development of advanced industrial society has created conditions for conflict that have gone and are still going beyond the control of established institutions. And as stability erodes, established institutions are scrutinized, as are other aspects of life that drew little attention in times of political tranquility. Submission to authority and conformity are challenged. The deterioration of the social infrastructure alienates members of the lower and affluent classes as well. Citizens heretofore complacent are politicized. Political institutions lose credibility. These are the developments to be examined in the present section. They are developments which can be checked neither by coercion nor the promise of affluence.

Dysfunctional Values

In the seventies the political support of a large proportion of the cultural stratum and of middle-class youth cannot be taken for granted. Public declarations and academic analyses alike frequently focus on cultural "elites" as responsible for the unrest and disorder among youth. There is some truth in Spiro Agnew's, Richard Nixon's, and Daniel Moynihan's assertions that the liberal establishment and university teachers are responsible for the declining support for governmental institutions among youth. Moynihan wrote to Nixon stating, "it has been said of America that the cultural elite will not approve that which the policy strives to provide. . . . The leading figures are going—have gone—into opposition once again. This time they take with them a vastly more numerous following of the educated, middle class youth, who share their feelings and who do not 'need the straight' world." [44]

For obvious reasons, the critical stance of this cultural elite cannot be disconnected from the over-all political and social processes, a relation which both Nixon and Agnew fail to grasp. What Moynihan does not appear to see is that the alleged nefarious influence of the "cultural elite" can exist only if those exposed to it have corresponding moral and intellectual predispositions. Youth, specifically upper-middle-class youth, have been raised in relative affluence acquiring social orientations that are contrary to the demands of a streamlined, rationalized society that administers people like objects, reduces them to dossiers, and permits only minimal participation in public decisions. If groups belonging to the cultural stratum withdraw their support from the political system, it is the logical consequence of their inability to neutralize their alienation by taking recourse in a plausible ideology.

The absence of a legitimating ideology leaves political and

economic institutions in advanced industrial society without a spiritual foundation. Daniel Bell has pointed out that entrepreneurial capitalism provided a moral justification by linking achievement and work to property. Corporate capitalism of advanced industrial society has failed to offer an equivalent justification. As Bell argues "the 'new capitalism' of the twentieth century has lacked such a moral grounding, and in periods of crisis it has either fallen back on the traditional value assertions, which have been increasingly incongruent with social reality, or it has been ideologically impotent." [45]

Without a moral foundation, the institution of work loses its intrinsic value. The protestant ethic provided motivational incentive, inculcated discipline, and inspired diligence. It made subjective subordination plausible in the name of a higher goal. Today traces of this ethic are more easily observed among the working class than among the middle classes, where values other than hard work for its own sake (or for salvation) are stressed. For several decades, the achievement drive appeared to be a viable substitute for Calvinistic goals, but as the analysis of the counterculture will indicate, the striving for social status and economic success (which at one time were proof positive of being one of the elect) has become suspect, especially among the affluent. The individual has to be motivated to accept the status that bureaucratic society accords him, which, as Weber pointed out in 1904, is essentially that of a cog in a machine. "The modern economic order . . . is now bound to the technical and economic conditions of machine production which today determine the lives of all individuals who are born into this mechanism . . . with irresistible force. . . . 'Specialists without spirit, sensualists without heart; this nullity imagines that it has attained a level of civilization never before achieved.' " [46] The absence of this motivation in today's society is evident. Most of the population perceive of work as a necessary evil and identify with leisure activities and recreation over which the state has very little control. The achievement ethos no longer provides the motivation to work for a great segment of the population. Work loses its function as an institutional source of cohesion. The rationalization of all types of work streamlines decision making in order to make it as predictable as possible. Strategies geared toward the maximization of investments and cost efficiency considerations reap profits for the few. A hierarchical organization of industries and institutions entrenches a pecking order not to be defied. These conditions are difficult to reconcile with emerging demands for individual responsibility, egalitarianism, and participatory democracy.

Because the organization of work in advanced industrial societies does not foster the actualization of these values, most of the counterculture has moved to the fringes of society, all the while infecting a limited, but nevertheless important, segment of the population. Communal and cooperative living arrangements, which in the late fifties were still considered temporary and insignificant aberrations of middle-class life styles, have become so commonplace today that they have ceased to be a topic of interest in the media. Sonya Rudikoff has estimated that close to 2.5 million Americans belong to the counterculture.[47]

There is no question that the refugees from society who live in communes have no direct political impact on the system. What is important, however, is the potential transfer of norms from the counterculture to society at large. In stressing individual responsibility within cooperative, communal arrangements and in their insistence on meaningful, noncompetitive work, the counterculture espouses values that are incompatible with the demands of dominant institutions. Those demands and institutions are scrutinized especially by the young. S. N. Eisenstadt has drawn attention to the scepticism of contemporary youth regarding politics and ideological promises. In discussing the direct identification of youth with moral values, he underscores the "awareness of the predicaments of moral choice that exist in any given situation and individual responsibility for such choices—a responsibility that cannot be shed by relying on overarching solutions oriented to the future." [48] Nevertheless, these values and the emphasis on morality are close to certain basic orientations of the population. The humanistic-liberal beliefs of large segments of the upper-middle class and their encouragment of individuality and innovation makes them open to the temptations of the counterculture, specifically if these values are not only preached but practiced as well. The population at large is more responsive to the quest for meaningful work and a sense of community than to calls for radical revamping of political and economic structures, although this quest, if taken seriously, constitutes a greater threat to the industrial state, capitalist and socialist alike, than does antiestablishment rhetoric.

A number of interests, at once genuinely social and firmly self-centered, countermine the concern for affluence and status. There is the interest in participating in the decisions that importantly affect one's life which is seen to include the state of a community as a whole. There is the desire to relate to the human and physical environments in a nonexploitative, constructive way. There is the need to express individual uniqueness other than through the dominant models society provides. And there is the need to avoid personal fragmentation imposed by multiplying and dehumanizing social institutions, some of which are meant to offset the limitations of the nuclear family.

When these interests cannot be pursued in the office, home, marketplace, voting booth, or local government, potential for conflict is bound to accumulate. These interests, marginal in the nineteenth century, motivate a large and expanding proportion of the middle and upper-middle classes in advanced industrial society. Increased productivity has created the material preconditions for alternative concerns and life styles, making obsolete those values necessary to conditions of scarcity. But even productivity is re-examined in light of ecological considerations which suggests that the environment is being not simply contaminated, but consumed, irreversibly.

Neither hedonism nor the generation gap can account for the coming into being of a counterculture. Bell, who has noted the decline of a moral justification for advanced capitalism, nevertheless pictures the counterculture as a phenomenon which "provides the doctrinal spearhead for an onslaught on the values and motivational patterns of 'ordinary' behavior in the name of liberation, eroticism, freedom of impulse, and the like" and suggests that "a crisis of middle class values is at hand." [49] If there is indeed a crisis of middle-class values in the form suggested by Bell, it would be no threat to the dominant order since it is relatively easy to adjust the institutional apparatus to spreading hedonism by removing restrictions on libertine behavior. Demands for meaningful work and effective political participation constitute not a challenge to bourgeois morality but an expression of it that threatens existent political and economic interests.

The reassertion of values and changes in normative patterns are endemic to any complex society. Parsons has frequently pointed out that the rapid change of advanced industrial societies requires a continual reorganization of the normative framework. He suggests that change is initiated in "large scale organizations, the development of science and technology, . . . the higher political processes, and higher ranges of culture" whereas the family and the school, the social structures that serve as the primary agents in the socialization process, are least likely to respond adequately to these changes.[50] This means to say that the individual may be motivated by norms and interests acquired in institutions which are not in harmony, from the point of view of the established order, with social development. Although in advanced industrial society these values and interests are mostly nonideological, they give rise to behavior which has political repercussions. By no means restricted to youth, they can be dysfunctional since they prompt expectations for which the institutional structure has no place. The growing demand among professionals for effective participation in the economic and political decision-making processes which has been studied by the French sociologist Alain Touraine, is a case in point. According to Touraine's analysis (which will be discussed in more detail at the end of the chapter) the bureaucratization and rationalization of advanced industrial society creates op-

position in the upper-middle class. As he argues "the new conflicts focus on the direction of society as a whole and arouse defense of self-determination." [51] In part, these dysfunctional values
and conflicts stem from the inefficiency of advanced capitalism
in the social sector.

The Sectorial Crisis of Advanced Industrial Society

The absence of a legitimating ideology and the inadequate reorientation of values contributed to the tensions experienced in
the sixties. During this period a sectorial crisis became apparent
which also served to exacerbate the decline of governmental authority by demonstrating its inability to cope with the problems
of the social infrastructure. This crisis came about because of
the overdevelopment of sectors considered to be essential to economic growth and military defense and the underdevelopment of
sectors which fulfill social needs only.

Health, education, welfare, and even the environment constitute
public interests which are considered secondary to economic
growth and are not as strongly represented through pressure groups
in the political arena as the interests of industrial/military sector,
both public and private. As shown in Chapter 3, economic determinants more often than not shape public policies in advanced
industrial society. Existing technological resources are not applied
to the social sector anywhere near to their fullest potential. Federal
resources for "private" industrial research and development come
forth more readily than funds for mass transit systems, neighbor-
hood health clinics, job training programs, and a host of similar
undertakings which are not and can never be profit producing
stimulants of the economy. Although the social sector was officially
recognized in this country during the 1930's, it is obvious that the
needs emanating from it are not met as thoroughly as those of the
military-industrial complex.*

---

* Defense related spending accounted in 1973 for 37.8 per cent of the federal
expenditures; 13.0 per cent went for community development, health, and
education; 30.4 per cent for income security; and 18.8 per cent was spent on
other areas.[52]

Military spending has increased continuously since World War II and rose in 1972 by $8 billion despite troop withdrawals from Vietnam.* In the same year the administration negated the spirit of the disarmament pact it had recently concluded with the Soviet Union by arguing that future arms reduction agreements require the construction of new weapon systems in order to maintain strength in disarmament negotiations. The staggering preponderance of defense- and growth-oriented spending by the government and the inferior status of the social sector is demonstrated by an abundance of data stemming from the social sector. A few will suffice. In the 1970's, despite current federal aid amounting to about $3.5 billion annually, close to two-thirds of the American colleges and universities, according to the Carnegie Commission on Higher Education, would be in severe financial difficulty, unless federal subsidies were augmented by $9 billion.** (The Higher Education Act of 1972, that establishes the right to college education for all Americans, increased federal subsidies by $2 billion annually provided this amount is appropriated by Congress and not impounded by the President.) The federal budget for 1970 allocated $2.3 billion for elementary and secondary education; $5.2 billion was allocated for ammunition alone in Vietnam.[54] During the sixties massive federal expenditures for Medicaid and Medicare resulted in the growth of a medical-industrial complex but did not significantly improve health care for the poor and the aged.*** [55] During that period, the United States was the only advanced industrial country where average life expectancy regressed.[57]

The over-all subordination of the social sector to the industrial/

* Increased military spending is, in part, obviously attributable to inflation. But it is worth noting that in 1972 close to two-thirds of the Presidential discretionary funds were allocated to the military sector and that the percentage increase of defense allocation for 1976 exceeded the rate of inflation.
** In addition, colleges and universities would have to cut their spending by $9.5 billion and raise $5 billion from foundations and other sources.[53]
*** As Barbara Ehrenreich and John Ehrenreich put it, "health is no more a priority of the American health industry than cheap, efficient, pollution-free transportation is a priority of the American automobile industry." [56]

military sector is reinforced by fiscal legislation favoring industrial interests. Reduction of corporate taxes by 50 per cent over the last twenty years has progressively decreased big business's contribution to the public revenue while government income from direct and indirect individual taxation has increased.* Because of fiscal policies introduced during the Nixon administration, such as accelerated depreciation rules and investment tax credits, corporate taxes will further diminish by an additional 25 per cent over the next ten years.[59] These policies were propagated as steps to ameliorate unemployment even though they freed industrial funds for investment in labor saving equipment, and most estimates indicate that the nonprofit sector of the economy will require greater manpower in the next decades than the profit sector.

The proportion of federal expenditures for Great Society programs, which rose from 2 per cent of the federal budget in 1963 to an estimated 14 per cent in 1973, seems to contradict the proposition that there is a growing disparity between the social and industrial/military sectors.[60] But most liberal and conservative commentators would agree that this spending has not substantially ameliorated problems of health, education, and unemployment, has not reduced social inequality, and has not reversed the course of urban and environmental decay.[61] This failure is due to the gravity of the problems and to the fact that a very high proportion of the allocated funds does not reach either the poor or the deteriorating social infrastructures but disappears in the financing of studies, proposals, guidelines, manuals, etc., and in the general administration of these programs. Nevertheless, the participation of the federal government in the social sector, though much of it is wasteful and symbolic only (viz., the pronouncement of grandiose goals), has significantly sharpened public perception of the disparity in sectorial development. The institutionalization of social rights in the areas of housing, legal services, employment,

* In the period from 1960 to 1974, federal receipts from corporate taxation decreased from 23.2 to 14.6 per cent of the total revenue. Receipts from individual income taxes rose from 44.0 to 44.9.[58]

education, and economic equality for women has opened a Pandora's box of expectations that realistically cannot be met without a lowering of middle- and upper-class standards of living.* What is important here is that aspirations that are not met undermine the credibility and authority of government. The political system may indeed need the mechanisms suggested by Luhmann to restructure expectations. But so far they are only part of the sociological and bureaucratic imagination and do not yet belong to the instrumentarium of politics.

The reallocation of resources from the military to the social sector is often proposed as a remedy for social problems. But commitments of future revenues, the failure of past legislative attempts to cut significantly the military budget, and the dependence of much of the industrial sector on the military would argue against the workability in the near future of such a policy. It is also possible to argue that the disparity can be reduced through further economic growth and through a revision of the tax structure. It was the rapid economic growth of the sixties that created the surplus necessary to underwrite social programs,** but since the economy of advanced industrial society is becoming labor intensive due to the expansion of the service sector, the productivity of which cannot be increased as readily as in the industrial sector, the growth rates of the seventies will, with all likelihood, be smaller than those of the sixties.*** If this is the case, revenue will not increase as rapidly as it did in the past and proportionately fewer funds will be available for the social sector. The extension

* Existing institutions, despite the productivity of advanced industrial society, are not structurally capable of meeting these expectations in the near future. To put it extremely, a nation of college graduates with the right to draw adequate compensation if unemployed and to live in an unpolluted environment is a utopian vision, even though it would be the logical extension of the right to higher education and the desirability of a clean environment.

** From 1960 to 1970 federal receipts grew by more than 100 per cent.[62]

*** The extent of the shift becomes apparent in the changing composition of the labor force. By 1980, 70 per cent of the working population will be employed in the service sector while 30 per cent will be employed in the industrial sector, a relation that is the reverse of what it was in the beginning of the century.

of existing social programs and the introduction of new ones is therefore doubtful. As far as a change in the taxation structure is concerned, a complete revision could free funds for the social sector, but the bulk of the needed additional revenue would come from greater taxation of the middle classes and upper segments of the working class. The outlook for the social sector might change if the political and economic ramifications of the redistribution of wealth (ownership of corporate stocks, mortgages, United States government, state and local bonds, etc.) were discussed. Any redistribution of wealth would obviously invite the well-financed opposition of the 2.5 per cent of the population that owns 45 per cent of the nation's wealth.[63] But even the redistribution of wealth and of corporate profits is not an answer to social problems since it would add little to the average income or property of the American.* It would significantly reduce the political impact of those groups whose wealth now determines their ability to influence communication and decisions regarding the solution of social problems. Barring that, it seems that in all probability, the gap between the social and industrial/military sectors will grow and that the potential for conflict will further increase.

No significant problems arise as long as the lower classes suffer alone from the consequences of the underdeveloped social sector. The overdevelopment of the industrial/military sector has made for affluence among the middle classes. Continued economic growth satisfies newly cultivated material needs. But the middle classes are also vulnerable to the consequences of the deterioration of the social infrastructure. Until fairly recently, noise, pollution, crime, poor transportation, major illnesses, and inferior quality of

---

* If all of the privately held wealth were distributed equally among all residents of the United States, each individual would receive little over $4000. Computed from census data of 1962, the last year for which statistics on the total amount of privately held wealth are available.[64] A distribution of corporate profits would not change the picture either. Susan P. Lee and Peter Passel point out that "redistributing monopoly profit would shift only about 1 per cent of income. . . . Total elimination of monopoly profit, even if every penny were diverted to poor people, would do relatively little to alter the lives of the bottom quarter of the population." [65]

schools were not problems for the middle classes since affluence permitted accommodation, as in the escape to the suburbs. Avoidance is no longer successful since these areas are beset by the very problems the working and lower classes have long endured. Deprivation is no longer horizontal; it is vertical, cutting from the upper middle class to the lowest social strata.

These deprivations might be regarded as the proletarization of segments of the middle classes, but that proletarization is hardly acceptable to those concerned. It is difficult to imagine any political justification of existing sectorial disparities that would make their consequences tolerable from the point of view of the middle classes, especially if no integrating ideology is available to justify them and if the government spends heavily on socially irrelevant projects such as the military and space programs. The educational background and the political sensitivity of middle-class groups makes them perceive social and environmental problems as defects of the system rather than as temporary political aberrations. It is inevitable that the quality of the political system is questioned by members of the middle classes.

Politization of Everyday Life

The articulation of demands, to reiterate, presupposes a political consciousness, that is, the recognition of individual and group problems as political ones. This recognition is the first step of individual politization. The number of people who come to such recognition is proportionately related to the vulnerability of the status quo. A depoliticized public perceives of politics as essentially a ritual and does not look for political solutions to whatever problems beset society. During the forties and fifties the sclerosis of political institutions, as seen in the decline of legislative bodies and political parties, combined with an seeming disinterest of the population in politics, suggested that the public of the United States was politically complacent. But while legislative institutions lost their importance, political issues erupted in other areas, institutional and quotidian. The intervention of the state into the economy, education, and social services, which affect most of an individual's life, as well as direct regulations such as taxation or civil rights legislation (extending or infringing them as the case may be) lead to the politization of everyday life.

The everyday relation between the individual and the structures of domination during the nineteenth century subjected citizens in comparatively few areas to the authority of the state. In today's advanced industrial society the state has become the fulcrum of society making all institutional areas (with the exception of leisure) directly or indirectly dependent on it. Directive legislation, federal regulations, subsidies, government contracts, and the tremendous growth of the state's administrative apparatus have narrowed the realm open to unfettered private initiative. Collective bargaining is subject to governmental regulations; fewer and fewer institutions are strictly private. The question of personal autonomy is no longer understood as entirely a private one to be resolved in the sphere of one's life, as neither are educational and occupational achievement considered strictly a function of individual merit. Today a more realistic understanding stresses the social ingredients of achievement such as economic status, ethnic background, and, most importantly, opportunity, which the state is expected to furnish, at least in part. Both the requirements of economic growth and the modest adoption of the principle of distributive justice at the state level have resulted in federal intervention and its attendant politicizing consequences. In the social sector, the increase of governmental responsibility has paralleled the institutionalization of social rights.

It is the dissolution of the borderline between the private and public realms that politicizes everyday life. Discontent over access to education and meaningful work, social discrimination, the quality of urban life, pollution of the environment, inflation, unemployment, taxation, transportation, medical costs—in short, the entire spectrum of the sectorial crisis—has found an easily defined locus since the state and "politics" are held responsible. Because the life of an individual is greatly affected by political decisions in most of the activities he pursues, it is possible for him to establish a relation between privately experienced deprivation and publically exercised power. The paramount influence of the political realm produces the expectation that the government remove sources of discontent. The overarching presence of the government in the economic and social sectors and the institutionalization of social rights provide a normative justification for governmental remedies. The perennial evidence of productivity in advanced industrial society and the public knowledge of virtually unlimited government spending for military projects and space exploration no longer permit the facile dismissal of social demands as unrealistic. Not only are these demands considered to be legitimate but, with reason or not, individuals and groups believe the government to be capable of meeting these demands.

Once the structural source of deprivation is perceived as the political allocation of resources, an important condition for conflict has developed. The transformation of demands for self-determination, equality, and a cooperative rather than a competitive relation to society, into political demands becomes the logical consequence of the changes advanced industrial society has experienced over the last decades. The more the citizen experiences his life as directed by forces beyond his control or as depending on outside agencies, the more he will hold these forces responsible for what happens to him. Failure is no longer simply a question of individual ability or lack of application, but understood, justifiably or not, as caused, at least in part, by society at large. As Ted R. Gurr has observed, a "striking characteristic of civil strife in the contemporary world is the extent to which its participants have political motives and direct their demands at political targets." [66] More than ever supportive attitudes and the loyalty of the masses can be sustained only if burgeoning expectations, partially a result of, paradoxically, political rhetoric and governmental participation in the economic and social sectors, can be met. However, the government's ability to do so is, as we have seen, considerably handicapped.

The degree of politization resulting from governmental intervention and unmet expectations is obviously not uniform, nor are
the responses of the political system to the demands it unwittingly
cultivates consistent. The type of deprivations contended, varying
degrees of familiarity with the structures of the political system,
access to interpretations with which to articulate discontent, and
the strategic position of a group are deciding factors regarding the
degree of politization of the group, the nature of the demands, and
the responses of the political system to these demands. Continued
economic growth, even if the rate of it declines, and the powerless
position of the most deprived groups make it likely that material
demands can be met. Declining growth rates in the middle seventies, though resulting for the first time since 1946 in a reduction of
the real gross national product and in significant increases of unemployment, did not lead to unrest among those groups concerned
since sufficient compensatory benefits were institutionalized by the
Ford Administration.* However, a serious conflict could arise if
a group that is in a decisive strategic position becomes politicized
and articulates demands that cannot be met with the promise of
greater affluence. Conflict is inevitable if these demands run
counter to the organizing principles of advanced capitalism and
if the legitimacy of the political authority to which these demands
are addressed is seriously questioned.

Delegitimation in American Politics

Governmental control of institutional areas and the resulting influence on everyday life subjects the members of a political community to an arbitrary allocation of resources and to decisions
which are binding. That is to say they are legally binding, having
been made by the established authorities, but their execution is
dependent upon voluntary compliance. Compliance presupposes
belief in a political system's legitimacy, a belief that must be passed

---

* Revision of income tax policies and an increase in unemployment benefits
that exceeded increases in military expenditures, offset potential repercussions
of an unemployment rate that had reached 8.2 per cent by March 1975 and
was projected to grow further.[67]

on to each new generation and reaffirmed in older ones.* As Easton suggests, the inculcation of legitimating beliefs applies as much to "adults who are well-entrenched members of a system" as it does to children.[68] The unequal distribution of resources can be justified only by a system of domination that is held to be legitimate. Where there is an obviously unequal distribution of wealth, the need for legitimating beliefs is felt more acutely in periods of affluence, particularly if the legitimating ideology is losing ground and new integrating rationales prove to be ineffective.

The decline of traditional legitimating ideologies creates a situation where the exercise of political authority becomes problematic. Voluntary submission to decisions cannot be taken for granted. Technocratic legitimation, based on efficiency and lacking the normative and evocative power as well as the plausibility of traditional modes of legitimation, is meant to replace these traditional modes. If domination is no longer rooted in plausible, acceptable legitimating beliefs which are engrained in the motivational structure of the public, a *process of delegitimation* sets in. This process signifies, apart from the obvious erosion of political authority, that the loyalty of the citizens to their institutions declines and that they are less reluctant to support extra-legal and even illegal means to reach political goals. Most importantly citizens will welcome structural changes of the political system if their demands cannot be met. The delegitimation of governmental authority is probably the most important condition for political conflict.

Trust in a political system presupposes that the system is credible to the individual. At one time this credibility was derived from ideologies, be they political belief systems or religions,

---

* It follows the logic of our analysis that the need for legitimating beliefs in advanced industrial society parallels the growth of governmental power and responsibility. For Easton, however, this phenomenon, though acknowledged, is surprising.

which either justified social discrepancies or envisioned future solutions to personal and societal problems. Today this hope-inducing component of the political system is no longer meaningful to many citizens. The political process, as embodied in institutions and policies, transpires without the mystifying mediation of an overarching belief system. The absence of a collectively shared, explanatory ideology, instead of marking the abatement of fundamental conflicts in society as it has been commonly assumed, has made conflicts more visible. If ideologies decline, societies become more transparent. Instead of being preoccupied with rationalizations taken seriously or distant but reassuring goals, the individual takes a less romantic view. Society becomes a concrete reality; its conflicts and inequities are no longer "ideologized," but perceived and experienced as such.

In the technocratic legitimation there are the assumptions that (1) individual values can be adjusted by political institutions to accommodate whatever values are required for the administration of a highly complex society and that (2) given this possibility the system is to be paid a blank check of allegiance. That these assumptions are dubious was evident in the discussion of the persistence of traditional values and the emergence of a counterculture. What is more significant is that the technocratic legitimation does not provide the subjective motivation necessary for voluntary submission to a political order. As Habermas has demonstrated in his critique of Luhmann, it is a sociological absurdity to assume that in the absence of either traditional legitimation or coercion, political decisions will be accepted if there is no other incentive to do so. Administrative procedures are hardly sufficient substitutes for legitimating principles since "the permanent acceptance of domination cannot be insured by legality alone if there is no legitimating rationale independent of the legal exercise of power." [69] Legitimacy must antedate the law. Easton argues a similar position when he suggests that successful legitimation presupposes an effective ideology and that the function of such an ideology is precisely the generation of socially and politically motivating symbols.* [70]

Legitimation which is based on material benefits and future technocratic solutions to social problems offers a pallid inducement for voluntary submission to a political order. Nevertheless it appeared to have stabilized the political system over the last decades. What was crucial for the support of governmental authority and institutions was the belief that they worked and could deliver what they promised. American pragmatism, transformed by the twentieth century, became a preference for efficiency. Success became more important for the general approval of a given policy than the nature of its conception and implementation.

If a political system is legitimated by efficiency and compliance is attained through material and social compensations, the distant, abstract nature of legitimating principles is nullified. Neither God nor self-evident truths, charismatic leaders nor the law, are as close to the individual as the regular collection of his trash, air that requires no effort to breathe, the freedom to walk the streets unarmed, or a war that is either won or terminated. When dysfunctions proliferate, members of a political community are prompted to examine closely the claim of efficiency. The credibility of the claim erodes if the political system is steadily subject to disjunctions. If opposition and discontent cannot be managed and if failures of domestic and foreign policy become public knowledge, skepticism spreads. Ultimately the very legitimacy of a system is questioned, particularly when expectations of major groups in society are not met over a period of time.[72] Wilson C. McWilliams has commented that a political system borrows its legitimacy if it is legitimated by expectations (regarding the resolution of societal problems) and faces "political foreclosure

---

* "The emotional roots of the appeal found in a vision of life, society and politics lie in the capacity of the belief system to establish a firm link with the motivational structure of the members in the system: to their conception and feelings about their own needs, interests and place in the political and social system or to their conviction that the ideology correctly and truthfully explains the real world." [71]

and eventual bankruptcy" if it cannot meet these expectations.[73] But even if these expectations could be met, loyalty to a political order based on expediency alone, is less compelling than one based on a legitimating ideology.

Unmet expectations emanating from a traditional understanding of the democratic process and the escalation of demands stimulated by a changing perception of needs are fundamental sources of current political discontent. The dominant institutions are no longer stabilized by generally shared, supportive political and cultural norms. This state proceeds from the hiatus between the democratic sentiment that one should have a say in the decisions that affect one's life and advanced capitalist society's requirement of reducing individual and mass political participation in the name of efficient administration. Concentration of power and the growing preponderance of the executive over the judicial and legislative branches of government runs counter to the democratic predisposition of both liberals and conservatives (except for those in Congress). It does not matter that electoral participation in politics never had the impact the public might impute it to have had. What counts is that illusions about democratic procedures and the electoral process are being shattered. In that sense it is perfectly understandable that, as Robert Dahl suggests, "old patterns [of authority] are losing out, paradoxically, because old ideas about authority, particularly democratic authority, encourage demands for new systems of authority." [74]

A changing perception of needs combined with awareness of societal resources encourages the articulation of demands. The nonfulfillment of demands stemming from newly established rights (employment, education, adequate housing, medical care, etc.) which, therefore, are *legitimate* demands gives rise to the sentiment that the structure of the government is at fault.

There are several other factors which contribute to the process of delegitimation. The disregard for due process by individuals in positions of authority proclaims at best a disesteem for legally constituted procedures and rights and makes it difficult to invoke the law as the imperative for the respect of legal procedures and established institutions. Governmental subversion of laws protecting civil liberties, which required centuries of political oppression before being recognized as legitimate restraints on the power of the state, renews profound, colonial distrust of authority.[75] The corruption of the White House which the Watergate investigation revealed, bore out the public's apprehension of dishonesty among its leaders.* The trust of the governed is further undermined by inconsistencies in policies and contradictions between governmental rhetoric and action. The inability to openly acknowledge the failure of policies or to provide candid or even plausible reasons for failures is politically damaging at a time when success has become the legitimating yardstick. Whatever the inadequacies of the present electoral system, the government has to make its policies credible and its failures acceptable. Poverty, crime, plunder of the environment, the unequal distribution of resources, and failures of foreign policies are politically acceptable to the citizen if they can be justified or if solutions can be foreseen. It does not matter whether these solutions are found in the belief in the forthcoming miracles of science and technology, in the belief in Horatio Alger or nirvana (instant preferably), or in the opinion that the welfare system will accommodate the disinherited. If policies related to social problems are not credible and if the individual does not see the possibility of change, then it appears that those in charge fail their duties. In short, they are no longer acceptable as authorities.

Delegitimation is expressed in widespread cynicism regarding electoral procedures and political institutions and in the recourse to political violence.** In September 1971 "a majority of Amer-

---

* By March 1975 the group of former high-ranking civil servants and White House aides sentenced to prison terms for perjury, obstruction of justice, conspiracy, violation of civil rights, and other criminal offenses included an Attorney General, two members of the cabinet, an Assistant Attorney General, a White House chief of staff, a chief domestic advisor, two counsels to the former President Nixon as well as his personal attorney.

** "In the [presidential] election of 1968 . . . 7 million registered voters did not vote because they thought the election was meaningless."[76]

icans indicated distrust of every major institution in the country
—business, the press, the media, the old parties and government
in general all the way up to and including the Presidency." [77]
Early in 1972 the *New York Times* could wonder in an editorial
"whether a new rot has infected the American political–economic
system." In mid-1972 the level of disenchantment was higher than
at any time since 1968.* Forty-seven per cent of the American
people felt alienated from the political system; 68 per cent believed that the rich get richer and the poor get poorer; and 54
per cent were convinced that their opinions did not count very
much. [79]

Cynicism and alienation from the political system results from
the conviction that the traditional methods of bringing about
change no longer suffice and that the system is incapable of meeting the criterion of its legitimacy, that is, efficiency. The safety
valves for the control of conflict, such as elections, and the tactics
for diffusing conflict gradually lose their instrumental value. Delegitimation is then manifest in the belief that the system does
not work and that severe instability is immanent. As of 1971, 47
per cent of the population saw in national unrest a factor serious
enough to "lead to a real breakdown in this country." [80] Under
such conditions the political system has to restort to coercion
and repression in order to insure the stability of an order which
is no longer guaranteed by collectively shared political norms.
Such a strategy, if used without avail, would further discredit the
system.

The process of delegitimation demonstrates that the system of
domination, governmental authority, and the institutions through
which conflicts were once mediated, have themselves become focal
points of discontent. If legitimacy erodes, an important condition
for conflicts over the nature of the political order is fulfilled, conflicts which are difficult to control or institutionalize. No longer
restricted to specific shortcomings of the system or to the quality

* Arthur H. Miller reports that in 1970, 44 per cent of the population dis-
trusted the Government compared to 24 per cent in 1964. [78]

of individuals occupying positions of authority—topics of reform politics—attention shifts to the structure of the political system and the powerlessness of the individual.

Because it discredits dominant political values, delegitimation compounds existing conflicts. If authority and constituted rules are not considered legitimate, an important psychological impediment has been eliminated that hitherto restrained the articulation of dissent and opposition. From the point of view of the established order, the cardinal challenge becomes the management of a crisis of values. The gravity of this crisis proceeds from the absence of a legitimating ideology and the political system's inability to cope with structural problems. Because of the process of politization, public awareness of these problems is growing in spite of distortions in political communication.

Whether or not this process is an essential threat to the stability of the political system is too early to tell. It is clear, however, that the decline of legitimacy and thus of governmental authority removes one important obstacle to structural change. As Hannah Arendt has argued, no amount of coercive power can substitute for the normative power of authority.[81] What remains to be analyzed are the reasons for opposition to the economic rationales of the political system within that class on which advanced industrial society relies most: the upper-middle class.

POLITICS AND THE UPPER-MIDDLE CLASS

An inquiry into the social origins of political dissent in the last decade points to the upper-middle class as that segment of the population whose commitment to the established order seems less than secured. The socialization strategies, values, and language code of the upper-middle class make it the class least vulnerable to the constraints on communication imposed by the political–economic system. Its communicative patterns permit the articulation of needs and demands that go beyond those sanctioned by dominant interests. Because governmental authority is declining, this articulation assumes an importance it would not otherwise have. It exacerbates the absence of an effective legitimating rationale and introduces one more irritant into political conflicts. The upper-middle class is the technical and professional brain of society. In the long run, advanced industrial society can dispense with manual labor and even with the property holder, who no longer has an economic function in corporate capitalism, but it cannot dispense with the professional and technical intelligentsia.

Over the last twenty years the composition of the labor force has changed dramatically. White-collar labor is replacing blue-collar labor. The middle classes grow at the expense of other classes. This expansion of the middle class is more a result of the phenomenal growth of the technical and professional intelligentsia than the increases in the number of clerical workers and low-ranking bureaucrats. The shift toward educated labor, meaning some amount of graduate study, is a mark of advanced industrial society. The professional and technical intelligentsia has nearly doubled from 1950 to 1973 to account for 14 per cent of the labor force in the United States.[82] This impressive growth is due to the reliance of the industrial/military sector on the technical intelligentsia and the rise of a service economy dependent on the professional intelligentsia.

The upper-middle class is composed largely of the technical intelligentsia and the cultural strata discussed earlier, an important segment of which is the professional intelligentsia. The professional intelligentsia consists of professionals who are often employed by institutions in all areas oriented to what has come to be called the human service sector. The occupational distribution of this group ranges from the health services to urban planning and includes professionals as diverse as the teacher, lawyer, physician, psychologist, social worker, architect, and designer, and government employees in these areas, including some of the highest ranking appointed and elected officials whose first commitment is to their profession. The technical intelligentsia is easier to pinpoint since the place of employment of those belonging to it tends to be more concentrated. It consists for the most part of the technical and administrative staff of private corporations and governmental agencies.

The analysis in Chapter 2 of class-specific socialization strategies and values revealed that the middle classes are set apart from the working and lower classes by values that encourage the articulation of dissent and by the ability to engage in political reflection. Few would disagree that the complexity and problems of advanced industrial society are more easily grasped by those who possess this ability. Reflection is linked to factors which were shown to correlate with upper-middle-class status. It presupposes a distance between the subject and object. Language is instrumental for the interposition of distance. As distinct from the language code of the lower classes (including large segments of the working class), the language of the middle and upper-middle classes encourages reflective responses to political events.

Any significant change in the class structure has political repercussions. It means a potential redistribution of power. In this case it reduces the impact of all groups in the labor force which do not possess specialized skills and knowledge. However, the upper-middle class is far from homogeneous politically. The technical intelligentsia evinces, by and large, little opposition to the dominant political and economic institutions, whereas the professional intelligentsia has become more and more outspoken in its criticism and even rejection of these institutions. What has to be considered are those factors that account for the support the political system enjoys among the technical intelligentsia and the growing political discontent of the professional intelligentsia.

It would be tempting to argue that the respective supportive and nonsupportive attitudes of these groups are related to variations in socialization strategies. According to our previous analysis, flexible socialization techniques that are child oriented set the middle classes apart from other classes. These techniques allow for considerable variation; certain values may be emphasized, others may be disregarded. Educational achievement and social status can rank higher than say individuation, responsibility for one's actions, or concern for others and vice versa. Whether an emphasis on autonomy and critical reflection among professionals corresponds to child rearing patterns which distinguish the professional from the technical intelligentsia is difficult to tell. Unfortunately, the empirical studies reviewed in the analysis of class-specific socialization were not designed to measure variations *within* social classes. There are, however, two factors which seem to explain the divergent political positions of the middle classes, particularly the upper-middle class: the context of work and attitudes toward legitimating rationales.*

In his study of advanced industrial society, John Kenneth Galbraith demonstrated that the technical intelligentsia (which he calls the technostructure) adapts to the goals of the large organizations employing them. It also tends to support societal goals that are determined by private interests.[84] Whether it is the goal of economic growth, the priority of economic over social questions, or the rationalization of a decision-making process, individuals belonging to the technical intelligentsia see little reason for disagreement with corporate and governmental policies shaped by these goals. The context of their work is such that the technical intelligentsia have very limited contact in the pursuit of their occupation with different segments of the public and that they encounter less intensely the social problems to which the professional intelligentsia are exposed daily. The nature of their work makes efficiency, planning, and rationalization guiding criteria. Administrative order and predictability are indispensable. On the whole, the occupational values of the technical intelligentsia are strongly compatible with contemporary principles of legitimation.

The technical intelligentsia has become part of the dominant class since control of knowledge and information is becoming at

---

* Kohn has noted that "there is little difference in values and orientation between the employees of government, profit making firms, and non-profit organizations." But he did not analyze variations of values specific to occupational groups belonging to the same class nor test political values and attitudes per se.[85]

least as important as control over the means of production. Alain Touraine writes that in adhering to the goals of "development and progress, it [the technical intelligentsia] identifies the interests of society with those of the great organizations which, vast and impersonal as they are, are nonetheless centers for particular interests." [85] The expansion of the dominant group to include the technical intelligentsia gives new meaning to the traditional notion of class conflict. If the working class is supportive of the power structure and the lower classes have no power, significant political conflicts can erupt only between the dominant group and the cultural strata.

As noted before, it has become apparent that more and more educators, artists, and intellectuals are unwilling to glorify or justify conditions in advanced industrial society. Compulsory miseducation, alienation, and the shallowness of everyday life are recurring themes in their work. The erosion of support among the professional intelligentsia and all the cultural stratum is a symptom of a deeper lying malaise that is intensified by the context of professional work, specifically in the human service sector.

Professionals are expected to hold values beyond those of the pursuit of material self-interest. To profess originally meant to proclaim one's faith. The capable, conscientious performance of services and the disinterested acquisition of knowledge rank equal to if not higher than the goal of profit. These norms provide the criteria which the professional intelligentsia apply to their work and to their closely related societal experience. However, growing rationalization and planning of society reduces the autonomy of professionals. As Bennett M. Berger suggests, "bureaucratic organization continues increasingly to define the conditions of professional work. These conditions render such work less and less akin to the traditional model of the liberal professions with their emphasis on responsibility, personal service, and creativity, and more and more akin to the bureaucratic model of professional and managerial skills organized in a 'functional rational' manner—a type of organization to which professional norms can only be applied with great diffi-

culty. . . ." [86] Under such conditions the professional is faced with
the dilemma of whether or not to compromise his values, a dilemma that is rarely experienced by the technical intelligentsia. At
one time the professional could exercise his work without feeling
harassed by governmental regulations or influence. Most of the professionals of the rapidly expanding new upper-middle class no
longer have that freedom.

The human service sector tends to become politicized when supported by public funds. As governmental agencies intervene, the
participation of professionals in the decisions regarding their services is subverted. There is always the potential contradiction between the financial requirements of adequate services and administrative decisions based on cost-efficiency considerations* or whatever happens to be the political priority of the government. Concern for the quality of services which the professional is meant to
provide places him between the needs of the public and an essentially political administration of the services. The financial dependence on distant decision makers prevents the professional from
executing his work as thoroughly as his or his client's standards
demand. Certainly, professionals in the human services have always
had to rely on outside sources of support, but today the source is
more remote and less susceptible to the personal influence of those
dependent upon it. Nor is it as easy for the professional to lower
his standards where clients apply pressure to improve services and
in some cases influence the occupational future of the professional.
The growing idea and implementation of the accountability of the
professional to his clients rather than, or in addition to, a group of
other professionals or to administrators makes it difficult for professionals, when succumbing to discouragement and indifference,
to cloister themselves from their public and fail to examine the
quality of their services. The technical intelligentsia, on the other

* For example, the criterion of productivity, that is the measurement of
quantitative output per manhour, if applied to higher education squarely
opposes teaching staff and administrators since neither the number of degrees
granted nor students "processed" are an indication of the quality of education.

hand, are neither personally nor collectively held accountable for the goods they produce.

By carrying out decisions they do not make, professionals have become, to use Alain Touraine's term, dependent participants. As Touraine points out, "the groups which demonstrate particularly sharp resistance to the domination of technocrats, bureaucrats, and technicists are those who . . . feel themselves responsible for a service and whose activity puts them in constant touch with consumers." [87] The extension of social rights into areas of higher education, health services, housing, welfare, etc., and public expectations that these rights are met only strengthens this resistance to governmental institutions, technocrats, and bureaucrats since they are held responsible by the professionals and the population at large for the shortcomings of the social sector. It is, however, apparent that the values and norms professionals adhere to run counter to the institutional organization of professional work.

It is evident that the changing context of professional work shapes the attitudes professionals have toward political authority and legitimating rationales. The more information a politically relevant group has about existing societal conflicts and problems, the greater the need will be for a legitimating rationale that makes the status quo acceptable to that group. But this need goes unfulfilled for the professional intelligentsia.

The technocratic legitimation justifies the principle of the exclusion of the public from the decision-making process in the name of efficiency, an exclusion frequently opposed by professionals who want to preserve control over their work. "Efficiency" and economic growth in advanced industrial society provide a high standard of living and the satisfaction of material needs. But instead of attenuating social and economic disparities, constant economic growth seems to have aggravated them. A professional whose attention is drawn to these disparities and the resulting social problems will not be convinced of the merits of a political system by its outstanding technological research and industrial productivity, especially if they bring no benefit to his particular area of concern and if he personally witnesses the daily deterioration of lives that might be prevented were public priorities different.

Because of their values and their experience at work and in society, professionals in particular and the cultural strata in general are the groups most politicized. They have the power of knowledge, but their authority to use it is diminishing in the planned society. Their knowledge is not translated into policies since decisions are aligned with technocratic interests. The institutions they work for are being drawn into financial dependency on the state gradually becoming domestic colonies of federal agencies, a good many of which are allied with corporate interests. The professionals' conviction that they and their clients ought to be in control of the forces affecting their lives collides with the political and economic rationales governing advanced industrial society.

The strategic position of the professional intelligentsia and the entire cultural stratum amplifies their political significance out of proportion to their numbers, which are not inconsiderable. The dependence of the political system on the cultural strata to perform this function gives these groups a political leverage as well as the daily opportunity to act out of motives that do not fit into the technocratic equation. Although the political option is being exercised more and more, it hardly has been utilized anywhere near its potential as a force for change. But even if political activism were minimal, the crisis of authority would persist since political authority requires the constant regeneration of its cultural foundation.

CONCLUSION

The unparalleled wealth and productivity of advanced industrial society is managed by a political system that relegates the citizen to a passive spectator whose identity is cloaked in the freedom to consume and whose communication is subverted by forces beyond his control.

Distorted communication thwarts emancipation from dominant interests and politically prescribed goals. It precludes the recognition that legitimating beliefs of advanced industrial society rest on material and social compensations which deflect the articulation of needs that could threaten the stability of the political system. Distorted communication, whether directed, arrested, or constrained, interdicts the critical examination of the rationales invoked to legitimate a political system and of the values sustained by that political system. Certainly, distortions of political communication in advanced industrial societies of the West do not match the experience of Fascist or Socialist Germany, but arrested and constrained communication are factors which can successfully curtail structural change in contemporary society.

Consumerism and affluence serve as substitutes for self-direction and social responsibility. The productivity of advanced industrial society and the strictures of constrained political communication,

reinforced by the accommodative (and presumably lucrative) policies of the mass media and the pragmatic slant of education, eliminate any questioning by most of the population of those interests
that govern society. A de facto alliance between groups that control
corporate and political decision-making processes and the working
class creates the image of a politically integrated system.

Both the dominant groups and the working class have unwittingly become, however, dependent on a rapidly growing segment of the middle class whose support of the political system
is precarious to say the least. To be sure, this segment is not the
lower-middle class, the army of sales clerks and office workers that
is unlikely to ever rebel against domination and repression in
advanced capitalism, nor is it the upper-middle class technocrat
who has well adapted to the rationales governing advanced capitalism. Rather it is the members of the cultural stratum, which is
responsible for communicating legitimating values and principles,
who are opposing the dehumanization of the political–economic
system and withdrawing their support of it. No legitimating ideology neutralizes the values they adhere to, because none available
is acceptable.

There is no political system that does not need to legitimate
itself. System legitimating rationales will always be required where
there are policies that favor particular interests. In democratic
societies, a legitimating rationale cannot be imposed by force.
Instead, the public must be persuaded to voluntarily accept the
claim to legitimacy by the power structure. Traditionally, claims
to legitimacy were justified by collectively shared, political belief
systems. But today, there is no dominant ideology in advanced
industrial societies of the West, nor are there effective counterideologies which expose the nature of the political system's claim
to legitimacy.

The complexity of advanced industrial society has nullified the
plausibility of traditional legitimating and delegitimating ideologies
alike. Contemporary technocratic legitimation based on efficiency
and the seemingly neutral administration of society, appears

credible at first glance. It emphasizes material and social compensations which the political system indeed provides. However, the rationale of efficiency of technocratic legitimacy negates itself. Efficiency is apparent only in the administration of things, in military and economic development, while it is blatantly absent in the delivery of human services. Though clouded in the para-ideology of science and technology, the technocratic legitimation is transparent. It lacks the evocative power of traditional legitimating ideologies. It offers no transcendent goals that could motivate the population politically and civically or relate it to any dimension beyond the consumer confines of their daily lives.

The expanding power of the state along with the politization of institutions in the social sector and of everyday life have created a condition where legitimation of the unequal distribution of resources becomes more pressing than ever. Instead of being met, this need for legitimating beliefs is intensified by the delegitimation of political authority.

If no legitimating rationales come into being that are acceptable to the population, voluntary submission to political authority cannot be taken for granted and the use of force becomes necessary to insure some semblance of stability. As a corollary to this phenomenon, the cultural strata no longer regenerate the ideational and—ultimately—the motivational basis of political control. Instead they seriously question the norms that determine the exercise of political power.

The insistence on law and order in advanced industrial societies of the West clearly demonstrates the dilemma of political systems in search of legitimation. The very moment law and order becomes the dominant theme and constitutional rights are mutated or simply negated in order to grant more coercive power to the state, the political system's inability to solve those structural problems from which conflicts arise becomes apparent.

Coercion does little to mitigate political instability. Its use may in fact be the *least* effective policy to reduce turmoil. A more promising approach, as Ted R. Gurr proposes, would be the adoption of policies and programs that encourage the acceptance of political authority, that permit more participation of the citizen in the decision-making process, and that increase the services the state provides or supports.[1] Policies leading to the acceptance of political authority would be feasible in a society where the allocation of resources were unfettered by private interests and communication free of constraints. Neither condition exists in the United States or in the advanced industrial societies of Western Europe.

Because the state has little influence over the primary socialization process, the transmission of values which are dysfunctional for the operation of the political system goes relatively unchecked. The resultant qualitative needs and demands cannot be fulfilled. Niklas Luhmann and Talcott Parsons have argued that the rapid pace of change in advanced industrial society requires a continual normative reorganization of society and the adjustment of individual values to the needs of the political system. The cultural strata have not adjusted their values to those required for the planned, consumer society, nor has a significant proportion of the middle-class youth. Other groups have learned the message well of the acquisitive society and offer little resistance to political domination. Nonetheless, there is a gradual politization of the population stemming from its dependency on the state and the latter's inability to deliver some of the services promised. To date, the cultural strata including the professional intelligentsia appear to be the only groups whose opposition to the political system is of consequence. The withdrawal of cooperation by the cultural strata erodes the normative basis required for the cohesion and operation of advanced industrial society.

The productivity of advanced industrial society meets the demands for increased material compensations, thereby legitimating the political system for some segments of the population. Coping with qualitative demands for greater participation in the political process and for life styles incorporating social responsibility, individuality, and autonomy, is, however, an exceedingly difficult task for the political system. The transformation of quantitative demands among important segments of the population and the delegitimation of governmental authority are the two most fundamental sources of conflict in advanced industrial society. As Daniel Bell suggested, "changes in moral temper and culture . . . are not amenable to 'social engineering' or political control. They derive from the values and moral traditions of society, and these cannot be designed by precept." [2]

Traditional theories of political crises focused on economic contradictions or fundamental inequities the political system appeared incapable of removing or controlling. Capitalism has proved capable of surmounting these obstacles. In advanced capitalist societies riddled by affluence and poverty, the absence of effective legitimating rationales constitutes a problem to which the political system has no answer. It is precisely this problem that undermines a political system tenuously held together by material benefits.

NOTES

INTRODUCTION

1. Herbert Marcuse, *One-Dimensional Man* (Boston: Beacon Press, 1964).
2. Daniel Bell, *The End of Ideology* (New York: The Free Press, 1960).
3. See Robert Dahl, *Pluralist Democracy in the United States* (Chicago: Rand McNally, 1967).
4. Arnold M. Rose, *The Power Structure* (New York: Oxford University Press, 1967); C. Wright Mills, *The Power Elite* (New York: Oxford University Press, 1956).
5. Cf.Valdimer O. Key, *Public Opinion and American Democracy* (New York: Knopf, 1961). For a selection of readings arguing similar positions, see Edward S. Greenberg, ed., *Political Socialization* (New York: Atherton Press, 1970), pp. 19–64.
6. For a sophisticated model of a self-stabilizing system, see David Easton, *A System Analysis of Political Life* (New York: Wiley, 1965).
7. Quoted from the preinauguration memorandum which Daniel P. Moynihan submitted to the president-elect on January 3, 1969. Reprinted in the *New York Times* (March 11, 1970).
8. See also Maurice Duverger, *Sociologie Politique* (Paris: Presses Universitaires de France, 1966), pp. 13–18; Max Weber, *Staatssoziologie* (Berlin: Duncker und Humblot, 1956), pp. 27ff.
9. Hannah Arendt, *Totalitarianism* (New York: Harcourt, Brace & World, 1968), p. 136.

10. Hugh Dalziel Duncan, *Symbols in Society* (New York: Oxford University Press, 1968): "When differences become so great that symbols no longer possess a common meaning people turn to leaders who do create new symbols of community," p. 130; "The legitimation of authority is based on pursuasion," p. 200.

11. See the summary in, Sidney Wilhelm, *Who Needs the Negro?* (Cambridge, Massachusetts: Schenkman, 1970).

12. For a discussion of the institutionalization of needs in societies characterized by consumerism, see H. Brochier, "Les Besoins Humains," and E. Reimer, "Besoins et Institutions," *Esprit*, Vol. 36 (1969), pp. 870–75, 884–90.

13. Cf. Claus Offe, "Herrschaft, Klassenverhältnis, und Schichtung," Frankfurt: 1968, unpublished manuscript; and "Politische Herrschaft und Klassenstrukturen," in Gisela Kress and Dieter Senghaas, eds., *Politikwissenschaft* (Frankfurt, 1909).

14. Cf. Frances F. Piven and Richard A. Cloward, *Regulating the Poor* (New York: Pantheon, 1971).

15. Seymour M. Lipset, *Political Man* (New York: Doubleday, 1960), p. 77.

16. See the discussion of the prevalence of economic interests over military interests in, G. William Domhoff, *Who Rules America?* (Englewood Cliffs, N.J.: Prentice Hall, 1967).

17. Cf. Lipset, *Political Man*; Dahl, *Pluralist Democracy*.

18. Richard Flacks, "Social and Cultural Meanings of Student Revolt," *Social Problems* (Winter 1970).

19. On the necessity of reconsidering cognitive elements in political behavior, see J. Steintraeger, "Political Socialization and Political Theory," *Social Research*, Vol. XXXV, No. 1 (1968), e.g., p. 123. "In fact every effort is made to shy away from an explanation that would indicate that reason, however understood and however inadequate, enters into the choice of goals or shapes attitudes."

CHAPTER 1

1. Cf. G. Granai, "Communication, Language et Société," *Cahiers Internationaux de Sociologie*, Vol. 23 (1957), pp. 97–110.

2. Julius Laffal, *Pathological and Normal Language* (New York: Atherton Press, 1965), pp. 24, 25.

3. Ernst Cassirer, "Le langage et la construction du monde des objects," *Journal de Psychologie*, Vol. XXX (1933), pp. 18–44.

4. Noam Chomsky, *Language and Mind* (New York: Harcourt, Brace and World, 1968); Jean Piaget, *Language and Thought of the Child* (Cleveland: Meridian, World, 1955).

5. Susan Ervin-Tripp, "Language Development," in Martin L. Hoffman and Lois W. Hoffman, eds., *Review of Child Development Research*, Vol. II (New York: Russell Sage, 1966), p. 60.

6. Paul Chauchard, *Le Langage et la Pensée* (Paris: Presses Universitaires de France, 1965), p. 34.

7. E. Judson et al., "Reasoning as an Associative Process," *Psychological Reports*, Vol. 2 (1956), pp. 469–79, 501–7.

8. A. R. Jensen, "Learning in the Preschool Years," as quoted by V. P. John and L. S. Goldstein, in "The Social Context of Language Acquisition," in Martin Deutsch et al., eds., *The Disadvantaged Child* (New York: Basic Books, 1967), p. 171. See also, E. Newton, "Verbal Destitution: The Pivotal Barrier to Learning," *Journal of Negro Education*, Vol. 29 (1960), pp. 497–99.

9. Cf. Michèle Vincent, "Les Classifications d' Objets et leur Formulation Verbale chez l'Enfant," *Psychologie Française*, Vol. 4 (1959), pp. 190–204.

10. Aleksandr R. Luria and F. Ia. Yudovich, *Speech and the Development of Mental Process in the Child* (London: Staples, 1959); Joseph B. Casagrande and John B. Carroll, "The Function of Language Classification in Behavior," in Eleanor E. Maccoby et al., eds., *Readings in Social Psychology* (New York: Holt, Rinehart and Winston, 1958), as quoted by Ervin Tripp, *Language Development*, p. 82; E. Olim, R. Hess, and V. Shipman, "Role of Mother's Language Styles in Mediating Their Preschool Children's Cognitive Development," *The School Review*, Vol. 75 (1967), pp. 414–24.

11. Cf. J. Stalin, *Marxism and the National Question* (Moscow: Foreign Publishing House, 1954).

12. It has even been suggested that indigenous languages are unsuited for the language of modern institutionalized politics. Cf. P. Alexandre "Sur les Possibilités Expressives des Langues Africaines en Matière de la Terminologie Politique," *Afrique et Asie*, Vol. 56, No. 4 (1961). For a discussion of the language reform in China, see E. Pischel, "Riflessi Politici della Riforma della Lingua in Cina," *Politico*, Vol. 21, No. 3 (1956).

13. Karl Marx and Friedrich Engels, *The German Ideology* (New York: International Publishers, 1969), p. 19.

14. For a discussion of the relationship between cognitive similarity and communicative efficiency, see H. Triandis, "Some Determinants of Interpersonal Communication," *Human Relations,* Vol. 15 (1960), pp. 279–87.

15. Cf. C. Wright Mills, "Mass Media and Liberal Education," in I. L. Horowitz, ed., *Power, Politics and People* (New York: Ballantine Books, 1963), pp. 353–73.

16. Cf. Herbert Marcuse, "Repressive Tolerance," in H. Marcuse, Robert P. Wolff, and Barrington Moore, Jr., eds., *A Critique of Pure Tolerance* (Boston: Beacon Press, 1970).

17. Wartime censorship abated during World War II with a few exceptions. See the case of the *United States* v. *Kunze, Pelley, et al.,* which was argued in 1944.

18. For a bibliography of relevant material, see Theodore A. Schröder, *Free Speech* (New York: B. Franklin, 1969).

19. For a lucid exposition of this position, see Peter L. Berger and Thomas Luckmann, *The Social Construction of Reality* (New York: Doubleday, 1966).

20. A. W. Staats, "Language Conditioning of Meaning to Meaning Using a Semantic Generalization Paradigm," *Journal of Experimental Psychology,* Vol. LVII, No. 3 (1959); "Meaning Established by Classical Conditioning," ibid., Vol. LIV (1957), pp. 84–90. See also, A. W. Staats et al., "Attitudes Established by Classical Conditioning," *Journal of Abnormal and Social Psychology,* Vol. LVII, No. 1 (1958).

21. Richard Eilers, *Die Nationalsozialistische Schulpolitik* (Köln: Westdeutscher Verlag, 1963), p. 14.

22. Ibid., p. 135.

23. C. Berning, "Die Sprache des Nationalsozialismus," *Zeitschrift für Deutsche Wortforschung,* Vol. XVIII, No. 3 (1962), p. 160.

24. Victor Klemperer, 'LTI' *Die Unbewältigte Sprache* (München: Deutscher Taschenbuch Verlag, 1969), pp. 261–70.

25. The examples given subsequently are drawn from Berning's series of articles which were published under the title cited above in Berning, *Zeitschrift für Deutsche,* Vol. XVI, Nos. 1/2, 3 (1960); Vol. XVII, Nos. 1/2, 3 (1961); Vol. XVIII, Nos. 1/2, 3 (1962); Vol. XIX, Nos. 1/2 (1963). For a listing in English of the Nazi terminology, see Henry Paechter, *Nazi-Deutsch: A Glossary of Contemporary German Usage* (New York: F. Ungar, 1944). For an annotated publication of the proceedings of the conferences organized by Göbbels' Office of the Press, see Willie Boelcke, *The*

Secret Conferences of Dr. Göbbels (New York: Dutton, 1970).

26. Klemperer, '*LTI*' *Die Unbewältigte Sprache*, p. 29.

27. Ibid., p. 241.

28. Ibid., p. 226.

29. The examples are drawn from the *Presseanweisungen der Pressekonferenz der Reichsregierung des Dritten Reiches*, Sammlung Brauner (Bundesarchiv Koblenz), as quoted by Berning, *Zeitschrift für Deutsche*.

30. Cf. Frederick Williams, "Language, Attitude and Social Change," in F. Williams, ed., *Language and Poverty: Perspectives on a Theme* (Chicago: Markham, 1970).

31. "Soldiers Who Search and Dissent," March 16 and 20, 1971, WNET, New York.

32. Cf. Rolf Glunk, "Erfolge und Misserfolge der Nationalsozialistischen Sprachlenkung," *Zeitschrift für Deutsche Sprache*, Vol. XXII, No. 1/2, 3 (1966); Vol. XXIII, 1/2 (1967). Glunk's data have to be used carefully since they were obtained from material which was published in private diaries after the war.

33. Klemperer, '*LTI*' *Die Unbewältigte Sprache*, p. 227.

34. Ibid., p. 37.

35. George A. Miller, *Language and Communication* (New York: McGraw Hill, 1963), p. 269.

36. Cf. J. P. Faye, "Langages Totalitaires: Fascistes et Nazis," *Cahiers Internationaux de Sociologie*, Vol. XXXVI (1964), pp. 75–100.

37. For an official statement, see *Neues Deutschland*, Berlin (DDR), February 27, 1947.

38. H. Hecht, *Sprachregelungen in der Sowjetischen Besatzungszone* (dissertation), Berlin, 1961, pp. 56, 57.

39. As quoted by R. Jacobson, *Slavische Rundschau*, Vol. VI (1934), p. 327.

40. Joseph S. Stalin, "Aufsätze zur Sprachwissenschaft," *Wissen und Tat* (July 1950), as quoted by W. Richter, "Zur Entwickelung der Deutschen Sprache in der Sowjetischen Besatzungszone," *Europäisches Archiv*, Vol. XVIII (1953), Col. 6053.

41. Stalin as quoted by L. O. Reznikow, "Contributions aux Problèmes des Rapports entre Langage et Pensée," *La Pensée*, Vol. 21 (1948), p. 164.

42. Reznikow, "Contributions aux Problèmes," p. 164.

43. Wilhelm Schmidt, *Deutsche Sprachkunde* (Berlin [DDR]: Volk und Wissen Verlag, 1959), pp. 4, 6.

44. G. Korlèn, "Nachtrag zu Joachim Höppner," in H. G. Friederich, ed., *Deutsch: Gefrorene Sprache in einem Gefrorenen Land* (Berlin: Literarisches Colloqium, 1964), p. 153.

45. Hugo Moser, *Sprachliche Folgen der Politischen Teilung Deutschlands* (Düsseldorf: Pädagogischer Verlag Schwan, 1963), p. 18.

46. Moser, *Sprachliche Folgen*, p. 9.

47. Werner Betz, "Der Zweigeteilte Duden," in *Gefrorene Sprache in einem Gefrorenen Land*, p. 167.

48. Ibid.

49. J. H. Greenberg, "Current Trends in Linguistics," in Peter B. Hammand, ed., *Cultural and Social Anthropology* (New York: Macmillan, 1964), p. 376. Morris Swadesh, "What is Glotto-chronology?," in M. Swadesh, ed., *The Origin and Diversification of Language* (Chicago: Aldine, 1970); Dell H. Hymes, "Lexicostatistics So Far," *Current Anthropology*, Vol. 1 (January 1960).

50. *Duden Rechtschreibung* (Leipzig [DDR]: Bibliographisches Institut, 1951), p. iv.

51. *Supra and Duden Rechtschreibung* (Mannheim [BRD]: Bibliographisches Institut, 1961).

52. Betz, "Zweigeteilte Duden," passim; Moser, *Sprachliche Folgen*, passim.

53. S. Pritzwald, *Osteuropa*, Vol. XI, No. 2 (1961), pp. 98, 108.

54. Wolfgang Schöfer, "Die Sprache im Dienst des Modernen Staates," *Sprache im Technischen Zeitalter*, Vol. 8 (1963), p. 617.

55. Werner Betz, "Sprachwandlungen im Heutigen Deutschland," *Merkur*, Vol. XVI, No. 9 (September 1962), p. 874.

56. Cf. Karl Korn, "Sprachwandlungen im Heutigen Deutschland," *Merkur*, Vol. XVI, No. 9 (September 1962), pp. 867–73.

57. E. J. Riemschneider, "Sprachliche Veränderungen im Bereich der Landwirtschaft," *Das Aulener Protokoll: Deutsche Sprache im Spannungsfeld zwischen Ost und West* (Düsseldorf: Pädagogischer Verlag Schwan, 1964), p. 91.

58. Moser, *Sprachliche Folgen*, p. 46.

59. H. J. Scherbaum, "Das Wort als Politisches Instrument," in *Das Aulener Protokoll*, p. 38.

60. A. Köhler, *Deutsche Sprache in Östlicher Zwangsjacke* (Berlin [BRD]: Spachenverlag Leben im Wort, 1954), p. 16.

CHAPTER 2

1. Hannah Arendt, "Totalitarian Imperialism," *Journal of Politics*, Vol. 20, No. 1 (February 1958), p. 25.
2. Murray J. Edelman, *The Symbolic Uses of Politics* (Urbana, Ill.: University of Illinois Press, 1967), pp. 120ff.
3. O. Brunet, "Le Nouveau-Né," *Bulletin de Psychologie*, Vol. 19, No. 244 (1965).
4. Cf. J. C. Daniels, "Social Class and Verbal Intelligence Test," *New Society*, Vol. 4, No. 86 (1964).
5. Peter M. Roeder, "Sprache, Sozialstatus und Bildungschancen," in P. M. Roeder et al., eds., *Sozialstatus und Schulerfolg* (Heidelberg, 1965), as quoted by U. Oevermann, "Soziale Schichtung und Begabung," *Zeitschrift für Pädagogik*, No. 6, Beiheft (1966).
6. C. H. Weaver, "Paternal Occupational Class and Articulatory Defects in Children," *Journal of Speech and Hearing Diseases*, Vol. 25 (1960), pp. 171–75.
7. Vera P. John and Leo S. Goldstein, "The Social Context of Language Acquisition," in Martin Deutsch et al., eds., *The Disadvantaged Child* (New York: Basic Books, 1967).
8. Ibid., pp. 166ff.
9. Deutsch et al., "Communication of Information in the Elementary School Classroom," in *Disadvantaged Child*, p. 218.
10. Martin Whiteman et al., "Some Effects of Social Class and Race on Children's Language and Intellectual Abilities," in *The Disadvantaged Child*, p. 330.
11. Cf. T. L. Baldwin et al., "Children's Communication Accuracy Related to Race and Socio Economic Status," *Child Development*, Vol. 42 (1971), pp. 345–57.
12. Ellis G. Olim et al., "Role of Mothers' Language Styles in Mediating Their Preschool Children's Cognitive Development," *School Review*, Vol. 75, No. 4 (1967), pp. 414–24.
13. Kenneth Clark [*Dark Ghetto: Dilemmas of Social Power* (New York: Harper & Row, 1965), p. 123] noted that there is a decline in the I.Q. from 93 to 87 from the third to the sixth grade.
14. Deutsch et al., "Communication of Information," *Disadvantaged Child*, p. 224.
15. Deutsch, "The Role of Social Class in Language Development and Cognition," *Disadvantaged Child*, pp. 360ff.

16. Deutsch et al., "Communication of Information," *Disadvantaged Child*, pp. 183, 182.
17. Deutsch, "Role of Social Class," *Disadvantaged Child*.
18. Denis Lawton, "Social Class Language Differences in Group Discussions," *Language and Speech*, Vol. 7, No. 3 (1964), p. 204; "Social Class Differences in Language Development," *Language and Speech*, Vol. 6, No. 2 (1963).
19. Lawton, "Class Differences in Language Development," p. 140.
20. Basil Bernstein, "Social Class, Linguistic Codes and Grammatical Elements," *Language and Speech*, Vol. 5, No. 4 (1962); "Linguistic Codes, Hesitation Phenomena and Intelligence," *Language and Speech*, Vol. 5, No. 1 (1962), p. 32.
21. Klaus Heinemann, "Soziale Determinanten des Leistungserfolges in Gymnasien," *Kölner Zeitschrift für Soziologie und Sozialpsychologie*, Vol. 21, No. 4 (1969). Heinemann's study has the shortcoming of considering only grade reports of students who succeeded in entering the next class. According to his statistics, the percentage of working-class students decreased from 20.3 in the lower classes (*Unterstufe*) to 8.5 in the terminal classes (*Oberstufe*), whereas the percentage for middle-class students declined by 3.4. The statistics covering working-class students are therefore strongly biased in favor of the more intelligent ones. The inclusion of all grade reports would have shown a stronger class-specific scholastic achievement and language differentiation.
22. Regina Reichwein, "Sprachstruktur und Sozialschicht. Ausgleich von Bildungschancen durch ein Künstliches Sprachmedium?" *Soziale Welt*, Vol. 18, No. 4 (1967).
23. G. Vincent et al., "Psychologie, Sociologie et Education," *Bulletin de Psychologie*, Vol. 20, No. 253 (1967), pp. 612–18.
24. Pierre Bourdieu et al., *Rapport Pédagogique et Communication* (The Hague & Paris: Mouton, 1965), p. 42.
25. M. R. Rosenzweig and R. Menahen, "Age, Sexe et Niveau d'Instruction comme Facteurs Déterminants dans les Associations de Mots," *Année Psychologique*, Vol. 62, No. 1 (1962).
26. Cf. F. Bacher, "Quelques Données sur les Aptitudes Verbales," *Bulletin de Psychologie*, Vol. 19, No. 247 (1965).
27. Pierre Guiraud, *Le Français Populaire* (Presses Universitaires de France: Paris, 1965), p. 79.
28. Ibid., p. 80.
29. Pierre Bourdieu, "Culture et Transmission Culturelle," Centre de Sociologie Européenne: Paris, 1966, mimeo, p. 123.

30. A. Strauss and L. Schatzman, "Social Class and Modes of Communication," *American Journal of Sociology*, Vol. 60, No. 4 (1955); "Cross Class Interviewing: An Analysis of Interaction and Communicative Styles," *Human Organization*, Vol. 14, No. 2 (1955). The table used is adapted from their articles. See also M. A. Straus, "Communication, Creativity and Problem Solving Ability of Middle- and Working-Class Families in Three Societies," *American Journal of Sociology*, Vol. 73, No. 4 (1968).

31. Strauss and Schatzman, "Social Class and Modes," p. 337.

32. Ibid., pp. 336, 337.

33. S. Ervin-Tripp ["Language Development," in M. L. Hoffman and L. W. Hoffman, eds., *Review of Child Development Research*, Vol. II (New York: Russell Sage, 1966)] reports that the conceptual hierarchies of children living in urban slums are retarded.

34. R. Cohen et al., "The Language of the Hard Core Poor," *Sociological Quarterly*, Vol. 9, No. 1 (1968), pp. 24ff.

35. Bernstein, "A Public Language: Some Sociological Implications of a Linguistic Form," *British Journal of Sociology*, Vol. 10 (1959), pp. 311–25; "Language and Social Class," *British Journal of Sociology*, Vol. 11 (1960), pp. 271–76; "Elaborated and Restricted Code: Their Social Origins and some Consequences," *American Anthropologist*, Vol. 64, No. 6, (December 1964), Part 2.

36. Bernstein, "Elaborated and Restricted Code," p. 62.

37. Bernstein, "A Public Language," p. 311.

38. Ibid., pp. 315, 317.

39. Ibid., p. 312.

40. Bernstein, "Elaborated and Restricted Code," p. 65.

41. Whiteman et al., "Effects of Social Class," *Disadvantaged Child*, pp. 323ff.

42. Deutsch, "Role of Social Class," *Disadvantaged Child*, p. 358.

43. Jurgen Ruesch, "The Tangential Response," in Paul H. Huch and Joseph Zubin, eds., *Psychopathology of Communication* (New York: Grune and Stratton, 1958).

44. See Martin Deutsch, "The Disadvantaged Child," in A. Harry Passow, ed., *Education in Depressed Areas* (New York: Teacher's College, 1963).

45. Bernstein, "A Sociolinguistic Approach to Socialization: with Some Reference to Educability," in Frederick Williams, ed., *Language and Poverty* (Chicago: Markham, 1970).

46. Bernstein, "Elaborated and Restricted Code," p. 56.

47. Ibid., p. 64.

48. Bernstein, "Linguistic Codes," p. 66.

49. R. D. Laing and A. Esterson, *Sanity, Madness and the Family* (Baltimore: Penguin, 1970).

50. Salvador Minuchin et al., "A Project to Teach Learning Skills to Disturbed, Delinquent Children," *American Journal of Orthopsychiatry*, Vol. 37 (April 1967), p. 559. See also Ann G. Skillmann, "Verbal Communication between Mothers and Sons in Learning Problem Families," *Smith College Studies in Social Work*, Vol. 34, No. 2 (1964).

51. Robert D. Hess and Virginia C. Chipman, "Early Experience and the Socialization of Cognitive Modes in Children," *Child Development*, Vol. 36 (1965), pp. 869–86.

52. M. L. Hoffman and H. D. Saltzstein, "Parent Discipline and the Child's Moral Development," *Journal of Personality and Social Psychology*, Vol. 5, No. 1 (1967).

53. Melvin L. Kohn, "Social Class and Parent Child Relationships: An Interpretation," *American Journal of Sociology*, Vol. 68, No. 4 (1963); "Social Class and Parental Values," *American Journal of Sociology*, Vol. 64, No. 4 (1958).

54. J. Jones, "Social Class and the Under Fives," *New Society*, Vol. 8, No. 221 (1966), pp. 935–36.

55. Leonard G. Benson, "Family Social Status and Parental-Authority among Adolescents," *Southwestern Social Science Quarterly*, Vol. 36, No. 1 (1955).

56. H. A. Witkin et al., *Psychological Differentiation* (New York: Wiley, 1962), as reviewed by J. J. Gallagher, "Productive Thinking," in M. L. Hoffman and L. W. Hoffman, eds., *Review of Child Development Research*, Vol. I (New York: Russell Sage, 1964), p. 366.

57. Gallagher, *Child Development Research*, Vol. I, p. 368.

58. Witkin et al., *Psychological Differentiation*, p. 3.

59. Bernstein, in *Language and Poverty*, pp. 40, 39.

60. Melvin L. Kohn, *Class and Conformity* (Homewood, Ill.: The Dorsey Press, 1970), p. 34.

61. J. W. Swinehart, "Socio-Economic Level, Status Aspiration and Maternal Role," *American Sociological Review*, Vol. 28 (1963), pp. 391–98.

62. J. A. Clausen, "Family Structure, Socialization, and Personal-

ity," in Hoffman and Hoffman, eds., *Child Development Research*, Vol. II.

63. Donald McKinley, *Social Class and Family Life* (Glencoe: Free Press, 1964), pp. 117ff.

64. See R. M. Stephenson, "Stratification, Education, Occupational Orientation: A Parallel Study and Review," *British Journal of Sociology*, Vol. 9, No. 1 (1958).

65. See R. M. Weinstein, "Children's Conception of Occupational Stratification," *Sociology and Social Research*, Vol. 42, No. 3 (1958).

66. F. Musgrove, "Parent's Expectation of the Junior School," *Sociological Review*, Vol. 9, No. 2 (1961).

67. E. Duvan, "Social Status and Success Striving," *Journal of Abnormal and Social Psychology*, Vol. 52, No. 2 (1956); G. Terrell et al., "Social Class and the Nature of the Incentive in Discrimination Learning," *Journal of Abnormal and Social Psychology*, Vol. 59 (1959), pp. 270–72.

68. Kohn, "Social Class and Parent-Child Relationships," p. 476.

69. See J. Newson and E. Newson, "Mothers, Fathers, Social Class," *New Society*, Vol. 2, No 40 (1963).

70. Richard E. Dawson and Kenneth Prewitt, *Political Socialization* (Boston: Little Brown, 1969), pp. 47, 48; David Easton and Jack Dennis, "The Child's Acquisition of Regime Norms: Efficacy," *American Political Science Review*, Vol. 61, No. 1 (1967); Anthony M. Orum and Roberta S. Cohen, "Political Orientations Among Children," *American Sociological Review*, Vol. 38, No. 1 (1973).

71. Kohn, *Class and Conformity*, p. 81.

72. Robert D. Hess and Judith V. Tournay, *The Development of Political Attitudes in Children* (Chicago: Aldine, 1967), pp. 256, 171.

73. See, for instance, Martin Deutsch and H. B. Gerard, "A Study of Normative and Informational Influence upon Individual Judgement," *Journal of Abnormal and Normal Psychology*, Vol. 51, No. 3 (1955).

74. Cf. J. Davis, "The Family's Role in Political Socialization," *American Academy of Political and Social Science*, Vol. 361 (1965).

75. Hess and Tournay, *Political Attitudes in Children*, p. 179.

76. Ibid., pp. 154ff.

77. See F. W. Koenig and M. B. King, "Cognitive Simplicity and Out Group Stereotyping, *Social Forces*, Vol. 62, No. 3 (1964); G. M. Vaughan and K. D. White, "Conformism and Authoritarianism Reexamined," *Journal of Personality and Social Psychology*, Vol. 3, No. 3 (1966); J. White et al., "Authoritarianism, Dogmatism and Usage of Conceptual Categories," *Journal of Personality and Social Psychology*, Vol. 2, No. 2 (1965); R. M. Frunkin, "Dogmatism, Social Class Values and Academic Achievement," *Journal of Educational Sociology*, Vol. 34, No. 9 (1961).

78. Hess and Tournay, *Political Attitudes in Children*, pp. 151, 154.

79. Herbert H. Hyman, *Political Socialization* (New York: Macmillan, 1969), pp. 31–35.

80. W. C. Becker, "Consequences of Different Kinds of Parental Discipline," in Hoffman and Hoffman, eds., *Review of Child Development Research*, Vol. I, pp. 192, 197.

81. N. Haan et al., "Moral Reasoning of Young Adults: Political-Social Behavior, Family Background, and Personality Correlates," *Journal of Personality and Social Psychology*, Vol. 10, No. 3 (1968).

82. Ibid., p. 192.

83. M. Gilly, "Influence du Milieu Social et de l'Age sur la Progression Scolaire à l'Ecole Primaire," *Bulletin de Psychologie*, Vol. 20, No. 253 (1967), pp. 802, 805.

84. For one of the most illuminating analyses of that process, see Pierre Bourdieu and Jean Claude Passeron, *Les Héritiers* (Paris: Editions de Minuit, 1964).

85. R. Castel, "Remarques sur la Démocratisation de l'Enseignement dans Certains Pays Socialistes," *Revue Française de Sociologie*, Numéro Special, Vol. 9 (1968), pp. 260, 269.

86. Gilly, "Influence au Milieu Social," p. 798; H. Peisert, *Soziale Lage und Bildungschancen in Deutschland* (Düsseldorf: Piper, 1967), p. 66.

87. A Girard and A. Sauvy, "Les Diverses Classes Sociales devant l'Enseignment," *Population*, Vol. 20, No. 2 (1965); Peisert, *Soziale Lage*, p. 67.

88. Girard and Sauvy, "Diverses Classes Sociales," p. 208.

89. G. Kath et al., "*Studienweg und Studienerfolg, Studien und Berichte*" (Berlin: Max Planck Institut, 1966), p. 111; Heinemann, "Soziale Determinanten," p. 833.

90. N. Bisseret, "La Naissance et le Diplôme," *Revue Française de Sociologie*, Vol. 9 (1968), p. 180.

91. The most important American study on the relation between social factors and educational achievement is James S. Coleman, *Equality of Educational Opportunities* (Washington: U. S. Government Printing Office, 1966). For a review of the literature prior to Coleman, see T. F. Pettigrew, "Race and Equal Educational Opportunities," *Harvard Educational Review*, Vol. 38, No. 1 (1968). Class-specific success rates are more evident in the humanities, nevertheless they can also be observed in areas where the cultural bias does not operate as strongly. See, for instance, R. Eichhorn and G. L. Kallas, "Class Background as a Predictor of Academic Success," *Journal of Engineering Education*, Vol. 52, No. 8 (1962).

92. S. Bowles, "Class Stagnation," *Transaction/Society*, Vol. 9, No. 8 (1972), p. 47.

93. A negative correlation exists between family size and I.Q. Since working-class families are generally larger than middle-class families this factor becomes important.

94. Ulrich Oevermann, "Soziale Schichtung und Begabung," p. 118; W. S. Neff, "Socio-Economic Status and Intelligence," *The Psychological Bulletin*, Vol. 35, No. 10 (1935).

95. Neff, "Socio-Economic Status," p. 729 and statistics in *Année Psychologique* (1960), p. 214. Both studies were done on English children.

96. See J. Abott, "Students' Social Class in Three Northern Universities," *British Journal of Sociology*, Vol. 16, No. 3 (1965).

97. A Girard and R. Pressat, "Deux Etudes sur la Démocratisation de L'Enseignement," *Population*, Vol. 17, No. 1 (1962).

98. J. S. Coleman, "The Concept of Equality of Educational Opportunity," *Harvard Educational Review*, Vol. 38, No. 1 (1968). See also F. Mosteller and D. P. Moynihan, eds., *On Equality of Educational Opportunity* (New York: Random House, 1972) and Christopher Jencks et al. *Inequality* (New York: Basic Books, 1972).

99. Reichwein, "Sprachstrucktur und Sozialschicht," p. 326.

100. Hess and Tourney, *Political Attitudes in Children*, pp. 126, 127.

101. Ibid., p. 161.

102. J. P. Shaver, "Diversity, Violence and Religion: Textbooks in a Pluralistic Society," *School Review*, Vol. 75, No. 3 (1967); "Re-

196   Notes

flective Thinking, Values and Social Textbook Studies," *School
Review*, Vol. 73, No. 3 (1965).

103. E. Litt, "Civic Education, Community Norms and Political
Indoctrination," *American Sociological Review*, Vol. 23, No. 1
(1963).

104. For an analysis of educational goals and institutions from the
Middle Ages to the nineteenth century, see Philippe Ariès, *Centuries of Childhood* (New York: Random House, 1962).

105. R. Queysanne, "La Réforme de l'Enseignement Supérieur de la
Fin du XIXᵉ Siècle," in Culture et Transmission Culturelle,
Centre de Sociologie Européenne: Paris, 1966, mimeo.

106. Jürgen Habermas, "Universität in der Demokratie—Demokrati-
sierung der Universität?," *Universität und Demokratie* (Berlin:
de Gruyter, 1967), p. 68.

107. Richard Hofstadter, *Anti-Intellectualism in American Life* (New
York: Knopf, 1963), p. 305.

108. Seymour M. Lipset and Everett C. Ladd, "The Politics of American Sociologists," *American Journal of Sociology*, Vol. 78, No.
1 (July 1972).

CHAPTER 3

1. As quoted from Supreme Court decision, *New York Times* (July
25, 1974), p. 21.

2. As quoted by Jack Anderson, *New York Post* (September 29,
1972), p. 30.

3. Gerald Ford's policy in this case obviously has precedents during
the Nixon Administration. Recall Nixon's refusal in August 1971
to provide the Senate Foreign Relations Committee with a copy
of the Pentagon's five-year foreign military assistance plan.

4. Alfred McCoy, "A Correspondence with the CIA," *The New
York Review of Books* (September 21, 1972).

5. The Pentagon account notes that at times the highest Administration officials not only kept information about their real intentions from the press and Congress but also kept secret from
the government bureaucracy the real motives for their written
recommendations or actions." *The Pentagon Papers*, Hedrick
Smith, ed. (New York: Bantam Books, 1971), pp. xxiii, xxiv.

6. Charles Peters and Taylor Branch, *Blowing the Whistle: Dissent
in the Public Service* (New York: Praeger, 1972).

7. Murray J. Edelman, *The Symbolic Uses of Politics* (Urbana, Ill.:
University of Illinois Press, 1967).

8. Murray J. Edelman, "Symbols and Political Quiescence," in Kenneth M. Dolbeare, ed., *Power and Change in the United States* (New York: Wiley, 1969).

9. Kenneth M. Dolbeare, "Political Change in the United States," in Dolbeare, *Power and Change in the United States*, p. 263.

10. Peter Bachrach and Morton S. Baratz, *Power and Poverty: Theory and Practice* (New York: Oxford University Press, 1970), p. 11.

11. Ibid., p. 44.

12. Peter Bachrach, ed., *Political Elites in a Democracy* (New York: Atherton, 1971), p. 7.

13. Percy H. Partridge, *Consent and Consensus* (New York: Praeger, 1971), p. 118.

14. Claus Offe, "Massenloyalität" (Starnberg: Max Planck Institute, 1971), typescript, p. 9.

15. James Chambers, "The Content Analysis of Two Newspapers to Determine the Existence of Class-Specificity," master's thesis, Hunter College, 1972.

16. Ekkehart Mittelberg, *Wortschatz und Syntax der Bildzeitung* (Marburg: Ewert Verlag, 1967).

17. Ibid., p. 46.

18. Henri Lefebvre, *Critique de la Vie Quotidienne*, Tôme II (Paris: Arche Editeur, 1961), p. 226.

19. Colin Cherry, *On Human Communication* (Cambridge, Mass.: M.I.T. Press, 1966), p. 210.

20. *New York Times* (March 5, 1972), Sec. 2, p. 1.

21. *New York Times* (June 4, 1972), p. 14.

22. See, for instance, the collection of essays, "Mass Culture and Mass Media," *Daedalus* (Spring 1960).

23. Melvin L. DeFleur, *Theories of Mass Communication* (New York: McKay, 1970), pp. 169, 171. Distortions in "high brow" media are reported in several comparative studies. See, for example, G. S. Turnbull, "Reporting of the War in Indochina," *Journalism Quarterly*, Vol. 34, No. 1 (1957); E. J. Rossi, "How 50 Periodicals and the *New York Times* Interpreted the Test Ban Controversy," *Journalism Quarterly*, Vol. 41, No. 4 (1964); G. Lichtheim, "All the News that's Fit to Print," *Commentary*, No. 3 (1965). C. C. Conway, "A Comparative Analysis of the Reporting of News from China by *Le Monde* and the *New York Times*, September 1967–September 1968," manuscript.

24. See Elihu Katz and Paul F. Lazarsfeld, *Personal Influence*

(Glencoe: The Free Press, 1955). For evidence from small group research, see O. N. Larsen and R. J. Hill, "Social Structure and Interpersonal Communication," *American Journal of Sociology*, Vol. 63 (March 1958).

25. I. L. Janis, "Personality as a Factor in Susceptibility to Persuasion," Wilbur Schramm, ed., *The Science of Human Communication* (New York: Basic Books, 1963), pp. 62ff, 58ff; N. Z. Medalia and O. N. Larsen, "Diffusion and Belief in a Collective Delusion," *American Sociological Review*, Vol. 23, No. 2 (1958); see also H. Cantril, "The Invasion from Mars," G. W. Swanson, ed., *Readings in Social Psychology* (New York: Holt, 1952).

26. Renate Mayntz, "Leisure, Social Participation, and Political Activity," *International Social Science Journal*, Vol. 12, No. 4 (1960), p. 574. For a similar argument, see W. Breed, "Mass Communication and Socio-Cultural Integration," *Social Forces*, Vol. 37, No. 2 (1958).

27. Karl Marx and Friedrich Engels, *The German Ideology* (New York: International Publishers, 1963), pp. 14, 15.

28. Ibid., p. 14.

29. Kenneth M. Dolbeare and Patricia Dolbeare, *American Ideologies* (Chicago: Markham, 1971), pp. 207–27. The terms "individualistic-conservative" and "organic" conservatism are suggested by Dolbeare.

30. Harris Poll, as quoted in the *New York Post* (June 19, 1972), p. 6.

31. Mostafa Rejai, ed., *Decline of Ideology?* (New York: Atherton Press, 1971), pp. 18, 19.

32. Herbert McClosky, "Consensus and Ideology in American Politics," in Dolbeare, *Power and Change in the United States*, p. 113.

33. Angus Campbell et al., "The Formation of Issue Concepts and Partisan Change," in Dolbeare, *Power and Change in the United States*, p. 143.

34. Jürgen Habermas, *Technik und Wissenschaft als Ideologie* (Frankfurt: Suhrkamp, 1968), pp. 48–104. This essay is included in a collection of essays: Jeremy Shapiro, translator, *Toward A Rational Society* (Beacon Press, 1971). Our pagination refers to the German edition.

35. Ibid., p. 90.

36. Ibid., p. 90.

37. Ibid., p. 64.

38. Seymour M. Lipset, "The Changing Class Structure and Contemporary European Politics," *Daedalus*, Vol. 93 (Winter 1964), pp. 272–73, as quoted by Rejai, *Decline of Ideology?*, pp. 19, 20.

39. Cf. Habermas, "The Scientization of Politics and Public Opinion," *Toward A Rational Society*.

40. Michael Lipsky, "Protest As a Political Resource," in Dolbeare, *Power and Change in the United States*.

41. G. William Domhoff, *Who Rules America?* (New York: Prentice Hall, 1967), pp. 90, 150ff.

42. U.S. Bureau of Census, *Statistical Abstract of the United States, 1973* (Washington: U. S. Government Printing Office, 1973), p. 233.

43. The statistics Bell cites for Europe were published in 1971 by the *Economist*; those for the United States were based on data available in 1970. Daniel Bell, "Labor in the Post-Industrial Society," *Dissent* (Winter 1972), p. 173.

44. See Herman P. Miller, *Rich Man Poor Man: The Distribution of Income in America* (New York: Crowell, 1964), Chap. IV. As P. Roby and S. M. Miller [*Future of Inequality* (New York: Basic Books, 1970), p. 37] commented, "the income revolution, touted in the 1950's as the graceful succumbing of inequality to economic growth has not occurred."

45. For an up to date summary of the conditions of the blue-collar worker in the United States, see Richard Parker, "Those Blue-Collar Worker Blues," *The New Republic* (September 23, 1972).

46. James W. Rinehart, "Affluence and the Embourgeoisement of Working Class: A Critical Look," *Social Problems* (Fall 1971), p. 159.

47. Alain Touraine, "Debat: l'Ouvrier d'Aujourd'hui," *Revue Française de Sociologie*, Vol. 2, No. 4 (1961).

48. Oscar Negt [*Soziologische Phantasie und Exemplarisches Lernen* (Frankfurt: Europäische Verlagsanstalt, 1968)] discusses the problem of the political education of the worker in West Germany.

49. See, for instance, Judson Gooding, "Blue Collar Blues on the Assembly Line," *Fortune Magazine* (July 1970). On the return to Taylorism in the same industry when productivity could no longer be attained through technological innovations, see Emma Rothschild, "GM in Trouble," *New York Review of Books* (March 23, 1972). An analysis of the underlying problem of

meaningful work is provided by Georges Friedmann, *The Anatomy of Work* (New York: The Free Press, 1961).

50. Cf. Joan H. Rytina et al., "Income and Stratification Ideology: Beliefs about the American Opportunity Structure," *American Journal of Sociology*, Vol. 75 (1970), pp. 703–16; McClosky, "Consensus and Ideology in American Politics," in Dolbeare, *Power and Change in the United States*; R. Blauner, *Alienation and Freedom* (Chicago: University of Chicago Press, 1964); J. H. Goldthorpe et al., *The Affluent Worker: Political Attitudes and Behavior* (Cambridge: Cambridge University Press, 1968).

51. See, for instance, the material on authoritarianism among the working class, in L. Lipsitz, "Working Class Authoritarianism: A Reevaluation," *American Sociological Review*, Vol. 30, No. 1 (1965); M. Seeman, "Powerlessness and Knowledge," *Sociometry*, Vol. 30, No. 2 (1967); Richard Centers, *The Psychology of Social Class* (Princeton: Princeton University Press, 1949).

52. Harriett Moore and Gerhard Kleining, "Das Soziale Selbstbildnis der Gesellschaftsschichten in Deutschland," *Kölner Zeitschrift für Soziologie und Sozialpsychologie*, Vol. 22, No. 1 (1960).

53. K. L. Specht, "Meinungsforschung in der Industrie," *Sozialer Fortschritt*, Vol. IV, No. 11 (1955). See also the comprehensive study by H. Popitz et al., *Das Gesellschaftsbild des Arbeiters* (Tübingen: J. C. B. Mohr, 1957).

54. Serge Mallet, "La Nouvelle Classe Ouvrière Française," *Cahiers Internationaux de Sociologie*, Vol. 38 (January 1965); *La Nouvelle Classe Ouvrière* (Paris: Editions du Seuil, 1963). This requirement is frequently linked to the proposition that only highly specialized workers are likely to engage in "revolutionary reformism" as suggested by S. Mallet and André Gorz. See A. Gorz, *Stratégie Ouvrière et Néocapitalism* (Paris: Editions du Seuil, 1964); S. Mallet, *La Nouvelle Classe Ouvrière* (Paris: Editions du Seuil, 1964). Specifically for France, there is, however, little empirical evidence to substantiate that proposition, as the author's research on the nature of labor unrest from 1965–68 in France indicates.

55. John H. Goldthorpe et al., "The Affluent Worker and the Thesis of Embourgeoisement: Some Preliminary Research Findings," *Sociology*, Vol. I, No. 1 (1967); *The Affluent Worker, Political Attitudes and Behavior*, pp. 76, 28.

56. Elisabeth L. Lyman, "Occupational Differences in the Value

Attached to Work," *American Journal of Sociology*, Vol. 61, No. 2 (1955).

57. O. Glantz, "Class Consciousness and Political Solidarity," *American Sociological Review*, Vol. 23, No. 4 (1958).

58. Harold L. Wilensky, "Class, Class Consciousness, and American Workers," Maurice Zeitlin, ed., *American Society, Inc.* (Chicago: Markham, 1970), p. 429.

59. Rinehart, "Affluence and the Embourgeoisement."

60. Georges Burdeau, *L'Etat* (Paris: Editions du Seuil, 1970). Burdeau defines the state as a system of domination determined by its functions rather than its origins, p. 19.

61. *U. S. Abstract*, 1971, pp. 305, 306.

62. For a "fictional" analysis with serious analytic overtones, see Anonymous, *Report from Iron Mountain on the Possibility and Desirability of Peace* (Baltimore: Penguin, 1968).

63. R. A. Gordon, "How Obsolete Is the Business Cycle?," in Daniel Bell and Irving Kristol, eds., *Capitalism Today* (New York: New American Library, 1971), p. 154.

64. See, for instance, Ralph Miliband, *The State in Capitalist Society* (New York: Basic Books, 1969); Claus Offe, *Strukturprobleme des Kapitalistischen Staates* (Frankfurt: Suhrkamp, 1972). Gerhard Loewenberg, ed., *Modern Parliaments Change or Decline* (New York: Atherton, 1971).

65. *New York Times* (March 5, 1972), Sec. 3, p. 3.

66. For analyses of the decline of the Legislature in the U. S. see David T. Bazelon, "Non-Rule in America," *Commentary*, Vol. 36, No. 6 (1963); Ronald Steele, "Is Congress Obsolete?," *Commentary*, Vol. 38, No. 3 (1964); Ernest M. Collins, "Congress Is Losing Its Grips," *Social Studies*, Vol. 57, No. 3 (1966); and Douglas I. Hodgkin, "Congress and the President—1968 Style," *Polity*, Vol. 1, No. 2 (1968). See also Mark J. Green et al., *Who Runs Congress?* (New York: Grossman, 1972).

67. This development is welcomed by some observers who even suggest that congressional authority over domestic issues such as the raising and lowering of taxes ought to be surrendered to the president. James MacGregor Burns, *Uncommon Sense* (New York: Harper & Row, 1972).

68. Henry Steele Commager, "The Misuse of Power," *The New Republic* (April 17, 1971), p. 19.

69. *The New Republic* (July 22, 1972), p. 9.

70. See, for instance, the background material in several Ralph

Nader Study Group Reports, specifically Robert Fellmeth's *The Interstate Commerce Omission* (New York: Grossman, 1970).

71. *New York Times* (November 12, 1971), p. 95.

72. David Broder [*The Party's Over* (New York: Harper and Row, 1972)] suggests a revitalization of the American party system according to the model of European parties as a remedy for the crisis in American politics.

CHAPTER 4

1. Abbé Papon, *Histoire du Gouvernement François, Depuis l'Assemblée des Notables Tenue le 22 Fevrier 1787 Jusqu'à la Fin de Décembre de la Même Anée* (London, 1788), p. 235.

2. Jürgen Habermas, "Theorie der Gesselschaft oder Sozialtechnologie? Eine Auseinandersetzung mit Niklas Luhmann," in Jürgen Habermas and Niklas Luhmann, *Theorie der Gesselschaft oder Sozialtechnologie* (Frankfurt: Suhrkamp, 1971), p. 258.

3. David Easton, *A Systems Analysis of Political Life* (New York: Wiley, 1965), p. 310.

4. Max Weber, in Guenther Roth and Claus Wittich, eds., *Economy and Society* (New York: Bedminster Press, 1968), Vol. III, p. 946.

5. Carl J. Friedrich, *Man and His Government* (New York: McGraw-Hill, 1963), p. 240.

6. Easton, *Systems Analysis of Political Life*, p. 278.

7. Hannah Arendt, *On Revolution* (New York: Viking Press, 1963), parts four and five; "What Was Authority?," in Carl J. Friedrich, ed., *Authority* (Cambridge: Harvard University Press, 1958).

8. John H. Schaar, "Legitimacy in the Modern State," in Philip Green and Sanford Levinson, eds., *Power and Community* (New York: Random House, 1969), p. 284.

9. Hannah Arendt, *On Revolution* (New York: The Viking Press, 1965), p. 194.

10. Philip Weintraub drew my attention to Georg Jellinek who emphasized that political institutions can come to exert normative power by their mere existence over a long period of time. G. Jellinek, *Allgemeine Staatslehre* (Berlin: O. Haering, 1900).

11. Henry Steele Commager, ed., *Documents of American History* (New York: Appleton-Century-Crofts, 1958), p. 100.

12. Weber, *Economy and Society*, Vol. III, p. 954.

13. Ibid., Vol. I, p. 33.

14. Ibid., p. 212.

15. Ibid., p. 36.
16. Ibid., p. 215.
17. Max Weber, *Staatssoziologie* (Berlin: Duncker and Humblot, 1956), p. 100.
18. Weber, *Economy and Society*, Vol. I, p. 214.
19. Ibid., p. 31.
20. Easton, *Systems Analysis of Political Life*, p. 396.
21. Seymour M. Lipset, *Political Man* (New York: Doubleday, 1963), p. 63.
22. Friedrich, *Man and His Government*, p. 243.
23. Schaar, in Green and Levison, eds., *Power and Community*, p. 288.
24. Niklas Luhmann, *Legitimation durch Verfahren* (Neuwied· Luchterhand, 1969), pp. 30, 38.
25. Ibid., p. 30.
26. Ibid., pp. 26ff, 11ff, 21, 24.
27. Ibid., pp. 28, 33.
28. Ibid., p. 35.
29. Ibid., pp. 26, 44, 145ff.
30. Ibid., pp. 151ff, 162.
31. Ibid., pp. 168, 191.
32. Ibid., pp. 192ff, 234, 235.
33. Ibid., p. 250.
34. Ibid., p. 225.
35. Weber, *Economy and Society*, Vol. III, p. 1394.
36. Friedrich, *Man and His Government*, p. 236.
37. Lipset, *Political Man*, p. 64.
38. Talcott Parsons, *The Social System* (New York: Free Press, 1951), pp. 26ff.
39. Ibid., pp. 27, 29.
40. Hans Gerth and C. Wright Mills, eds., *From Max Weber: Essays in Sociology* (New York: Oxford University Press, 1958), p. 280.
41. Suzanne Keller, *Beyond the Ruling Class* (New York: Random House, 1968), pp. 138, 140.
42. Ibid., p. 146.
43. Crane Brinton, *The Anatomy of Revolution* (New York: Random House, 1965), p. 251.
44. Daniel P. Moynihan, Pre-Inauguration Memorandum, *New York Times* (March 11, 1970).
45. Daniel Bell, "The Cultural Contradiction of Capitalism," in

D. Bell and I. Kristol, eds., *Capitalism Today* (New York: New American Library, 1971), p. 52.

46. Max Weber, *The Protestant Ethic and the Spirit of Capitalism* (New York: Scribner, 1958), pp. 181, 182.

47. Sonya Rudikoff, "The Whole Earth People," *Commentary* (July 1972), p. 65.

48. S. N. Eisenstadt, "Archetypical Patterns of Youth," in Erik H. Erikson, ed., *The Challenge of Youth* (New York: Doubleday, 1965), p. 49.

49. Bell, "Cultural Contradiction," p. 47.

50. Talcott Parsons, "Youth in the Context of American Society," *The Challenge of Youth*, p. 128.

51. Alain Touraine, *The Post Industrial Society* (New York: Random House, 1971), p. 63.

52. *Statistical Abstract, 1973* (Washington: U. S. Government Printing Office, 1973), p. 389.

53. *New York Times* (June 18, 1972), Sec. 4, p. 9.

54. H. J. Ehrlich, "Social Conflict in America: the 1960's," *The Sociological Quarterly* (Summer 1971), p. 296.

55. Barbara Ehrenreich and John Ehrenreich, "The Medical-Industrial Complex," *New York Review of Books* (December 12, 1970).

56. Barbara Ehrenreich and John Ehrenreich, *The American Health Empire* (New York: Random House, 1970), p. vi.

57. *Statistical Abstract, 1971*, p. 53.

Life expectancy in the United States is lower than in comparable advanced industrial societies:

	Year	Male	Female
United States	1968	66.6	74.0
Germany	1966–68	67.5	73.6
Sweden	1967	71.8	76.5
France	1969	67.6	74.9
Great Brit.	1967–69	68.7	74.9

Source: *Statistical Yearbook, 1971* (New York: United Nations. 1972), pp. 76–79.

58. *Statistical Abstract, 1971*, p. 373 and *New York Times* (February 4, 1975), p. 20.

59. Mark Green and Peter Petkas, "Nixon's Industrial State," *The New Republic* (September 16, 1972), p. 20.

60. *New York Times* (May 25, 1972), p. 32.

61. See Edward Banfield, *The Unheavenly City: The Nature and*

Future of Our Urban Crisis (Boston: Little Brown, 1970); Jeffrey K. Hadden, ed., *Metropolis in Crisis* (Itasca, Ill.: Peacock, 1967). For a critical examination of the failure of private and public rehabilitation programs, see Daniel P. Kennedy and August Kerber, *Resocialization: An American Experience* (New York: Behavioral Publications, 1972).

62. *Statistical Abstract*, 1971, p. 373.

63. Lester C. Thurow, *The Impact of Taxes on the American Economy* (New York: Praeger, 1971), p. 129.

64. *Statistical Abstract*, 1971, pp. 5, 327.

65. *New York Times Book Review* (September 10, 1972), pp. 31, 34.

66. Ted Robert Gurr, *Why Men Rebel* (Princeton: Princeton University Press, 1970), p. 177.

67. *New York Times* (March 9, 1975), Sec. 4, p. 1.

68. Easton, *Systems Analysis of Political Life*, p. 308.

69. Habermas, "Theorie der Gesellschaft oder Sozialtechnologie? Eine Auseinandersetzung mit Niklas Luhmann," p. 243.

70. Easton, *Systems Analysis of Political Life*, pp. 292–309.

71. Ibid., p. 295.

72. Lipset, *Political Man*, p. 65. Lipset restricts this observation to new political systems.

73. Wilson C. McWilliams, "On Political Illegitimacy," *Public Policy* (Summer 1971), p. 448.

74. Robert Dahl, *After the Revolution* (New Haven: Yale University Press, 1970), p. 4.

75. For a detailed discussion of the erosion of civil rights under the administration of Richard Nixon, see Richard Harris, "Reflections (Anti-Crime Laws)," *New Yorker* (March 25, 1972). On the question of the constitutionality of the war in Vietnam, see Alexander M. Bickel, "The Constitution and the War," *Commentary* (July 1972). For a review of governmental violations of the law in the 1960's, see Jethro K. Lieberman, *How the Government Breaks the Law* (New York: Stein and Day, 1972).

76. Ehrlich, "Social Conflict in America," p. 301.

77. C. Vann Woodward, "The Ghost of Populism Walks Again," *New York Times Magazine* (June 4, 1972), p. 60.

78. Arthur H. Miller, *Psychology Today* (December 1972), pp. 14, 15.

79. Harris Poll as quoted in the *New York Post* (June 19, 1972), p. 6.

80. Albert H. Cantril and Charles W. Roll, Jr., *Hopes and Fears*

of the American People (New York: Universe Book, 1971), p. 68.

81. Hannah Arendt, "Thoughts on Politics and Revolution," *Crises of the Republic*, p. 205.

82. The professionalization of the labor force finds its foremost expression in the expansion of higher education. The number of total degrees conferred doubled from 1950 to 1969 and reached 990,000. It is significant that the number of master's and doctorates granted rose to 22.3 per cent of this total and that graduate institutions expanded at a higher rate than undergraduate institutions. *Statistical Abstracts*, 1971, pp. 131, 126.

Composition of the labor force:

	1950	1973
Professional and technical workers	7.5%	14.0%
Other white collar	30.0%	33.9%
Blue collar, service and farm worker	62.5%	52.1%

Source: Computed from *Statistical Abstracts* 1973, p. 233.

83. Melvin L. Kohn, *Class and Conformity* (Urbana, Ill.: Dorsey, 1969), p. 172.

84. John K. Galbraith, *The New Industrial State* (New York: New American Library, 1968), pp. 159–68.

85. Touraine, *Post Industrial Society*, p. 53.

86. Bennett M. Berger, "The Sociology of Leisure," *Industrial Relations*, Vol. I, No. 2, 1962, p. 43.

87. Touraine, *Post Industrial Society*, p. 66.

CONCLUSION

1. Ted Robert Gurr, "Sources of Rebellion in Western Societies: Some Quantitative Evidence," *The Annals of the American Academy of Political and Social Science*, Vol. 391 (September 1970).

2. Daniel Bell, "The Cultural Contradiction of Capitalism," in D. Bell and I. Kristol, eds., *Capitalism Today* (New York: New American Library, 1971), p. 56.

BIBLIOGRAPHY

Abcarian, Gilbert, and Soule, John W., eds., *Social Psychology and Political Behavior* (Columbus, Ohio: Merrill, 1971).

Aranguren, José L., *Sociologie de l'Information* (Paris: Hachette, 1968).

Arendt, Hannah, *Between Past and Future* (New York: Viking Press, 1968).

———, *Crises of the Republic* (New York: Harcourt, 1972).

———, *Totalitarianism* (New York: Harcourt, 1968).

Bachrach, Peter, ed., *Political Elites in a Democracy* (Chicago: Aldine, 1971).

Bachrach, Peter, and Baratz, Morton S., *Power and Poverty* (New York: Oxford, 1970).

Banfield, Edward S., *The Unheavenly City* (Boston: Little Brown, 1970).

Bell, Daniel, and Kristol, Irving, eds., *Capitalism Today* (New York: New American Library, 1971).

Berger, Peter, and Luckmann, Thomas, *The Social Construction of Reality* (New York: Doubleday, 1967).

Birnbaum, Norman, *Toward a Critical Sociology* (New York: Oxford, 1971).

Bottomore, Tom B., *Elites and Society* (Baltimore: Penguin, 1966).

Bourdieu, Pierre, "Culture and Transmission Culturelle," mimeo, Paris: Centre de Sociologie Européenne, 1966.

Bourdieu, Pierre, and Passeron, Jean C., *Rapport Pédagogique et Communication* (The Hague: Mouton, 1965).

——, *Les Héritiers* (Paris: Editions de Minuit, 1964).

Brinton, Crane, *The Anatomy of Revolution* (New York: Random House, 1965).

Burdeau, Georges, *L'Etat* (Paris: Editions du Seuil, 1970).

Chauchard, Paul, *Le Langage et la Pensée* (Paris: P.U.F., 1965).

Cherry, Colin, *On Human Communication* (Cambridge, Mass.: M.I.T. Press, 1966).

Clark, Kenneth, *Dark Ghetto* (New York: Harper, 1965).

Cohen, Marcel, *Pour une Sociologie du Langage* (Paris: Albin Michel, 1956).

Coser, Lewis, *The Functions of Social Conflict* (New York: Free Press, 1956).

Dahl, Robert, *After the Revolution* (New Haven, Yale University Press, 1970).

DeFleur, Melvin, *Theories of Mass Communication* (New York: McKay, 1970).

Deutsch, Karl W., *The Nerves of Government* (New York: Free Press, 1963).

Deutsch, Martin, and Associates, *The Disadvantaged Child* (New York: Basic Books, 1967).

Dolbeare, Kenneth M., ed., *Power and Change in the United States* (New York: Wiley, 1969).

Dolbeare, Kenneth M., and Dolbeare, Patricia, *American Ideologies* (Chicago: Markham, 1971).

Domhoff, G. William, *Who Rules America?* (New York: Prentice Hall, 1967).

Duncan, Hugh D., *Symbols in Society* (New York: Oxford, 1958).

——, *Communication and the Social Order* (New York: Oxford, 1962).

Duverger, Maurice, *Sociologie Politique* (Paris: P.U.F., 1965).

Easton, David, *The Political System* (New York: Knopf, 1971).

——, *A Systems Analysis of Political Life* (New York: Wiley, 1965).

Edelman, Murray J., *The Symbolic Uses of Politics* (Urbana, Ill.: University of Illinois Press, 1967).

Ehrenreich, Barbara, and Ehrenreich, John, *The American Health Empire* (New York: Random House, 1970).

Eilers, Rudolf, *Die Nationalsozialistische Schulpolitik* (Köln: Westdeutscher Verlag, 1963).

Ellul, Jaques, *The Technological Society* (New York: Knopf, 1964).

d'Entreves, Alexander P., *The Notion of the State* (New York: Oxford, 1967).

Friedmann, Georges, *The Anatomy of Work* (New York: Free Press, 1961).

Friedrich, Carl J., *Man and His Government* (New York: McGraw Hill, 1963).

Galbraith, John K., *The New Industrial State* (New York: New American Library, 1967).

Glunk, Rolf, "Erfolge und Misserfolge Nationalsozialistischer Sprachlenkung," dissertation, München, 1963.

Goffman, Erving, *The Presentation of Self in Everyday Life* (New York: Doubleday, 1959).

Goldthorpe, John H., et al., *The Affluent Worker: Political Attitudes* (Cambridge: Cambridge University Press, 1968).

Gorz, André, *Strategy for Labor* (Boston: Beacon, 1968).

Greenberg, Edward S., ed., *Political Socialization* (New York: Atherton, 1970).

Guiraud, Pierre, *Le Français Populair* (Paris: P.U.F., 1965).

Gurr, Ted. W., *Why Men Rebel* (Princeton: Princeton University Press, 1970).

Habermas, Jürgen, *Erkenntnis und Interesse* (Frankfurt: Suhrkamp, 1968).

———, *Protestbewegung und Hochschulreform* (Frankfurt: Suhrkamp, 1969).

———, *Technik und Wissenschaft als "Ideologie"* (Frankfurt: Suhrkamp, 1968).

Habermas, Jürgen, and Luhmann, Niklas, *Theorie der Gesellschaft oder Sozialtechnologie* (Frankfurt: Suhrkamp, 1971).

Harrington, Michael, *The Accidental Century* (Baltimore: Penguin, 1965).

Heilbroner, Robert, *The Limits of American Capitalism* (New York: Harper, 1966).

Hess, Robert D., and Torney, Judith, F., *The Development of Political Attitudes in Children* (New York: Doubleday, 1967).

Hoffman, Martin L., and Hoffman, Lois M., *Review of Child Development Research*, Vols. I and II (New York: Russell Sage, 1964–66).

Holzer, Horst, *Gescheiterte Aufklärung* (München: Piper, 1971).

Hyman, Herbert H., *Political Socialization* (New York: Free Press, 1959).

Johnson, Chalmers, *Revolutionary Change* (Boston: Little Brown, 1966).

Kariel, Henry S., *The Decline of American Pluralism* (Stanford: Stanford University Press, 1961).

Kath, Gerhard, *Studienweg und Studienerfolg* (Berlin: Max Planck Gesellschaft, 1966).

Katz, Elihu, and Lazarsfeld, Paul F., *Personal Influence* (Glencoe, Ill.: Free Press, 1955).

Keller, Suzanne, *Beyond the Ruling Class* (New York: Random House, 1968).

Kennedy, Daniel B., and Kerber, August, *Resocialization: An American Experience* (New York: Behavioral Publications, 1973).

Klemperer, Viktor, 'LTI' *Die Unbewältigte Sprache* (München: Deutscher Taschenbuch Verlag, 1969).

Kohn, Melvin L., *Class and Conformity* (Urbana, Ill.: Dorsey, 1969).

Kuhn, Thomas S., *The Structure of Scientific Revolution* (Chicago: University of Chicago Press, 1962).

Laffal, Julius, *Pathological and Normal Language* (New York: Russell Sage, 1966).

Lawton, Denis, *Social Class, Language and Education* (London: Routledge, 1968).

Lefebvre, Henri, *Critique de la Vie Quotidienne, Tôme II: Fondements d'une Sociologie de la Quotidienneté* (Paris: L'Arche, 1961).

———, *Le Langage et la Société* (Paris: Gallimard, 1966).

Lewin, L. C., ed., *Report From Iron Mountain on the Possibility and Desirability of Peace* (London: Penguin, 1968).

Lipset, Seymour M., *Political Man* (New York: Doubleday, 1963).

Lubell, Samuel, *The Hidden Crisis in American Politics* (New York: Norton, 1970).

Luhmann, Niklas, *Legitimation durch Verfahren* (Neuwied: Luchterhand, 1969).

Luria, Aleksandr, *Speech and the Development of Mental Processes in the Child* (London: Staples, 1959).

Mallet, Serge, *La Nouvelle Classe Ouvrière* (Paris: Editions du Seuil, 1963).

Mannheim, Karl, *Ideology and Utopia* (New York: Harcourt, n.d.).

Marcuse, Herbert, *One Dimensional Man* (Boston: Beacon, 1964).

Marcuse, Herbert, et al., *A Critique of Pure Tolerance* (Boston: Beacon, 1970).

Marx, Karl, and Engels, Friedrich, *The German Ideology* (New York: International Publisher, 1960).

Merelman, Richard M., *Political Socialization and Educational Climates* (New York: Holt, 1971).

McKinley, D. C., *Social Class and Family Life* (New York: Free Press, 1964).

Miliband, Ralph, *The State in Capitalist Society* (New York: Basic Books, 1969).

Miller, George A., *Language and Communication* (New York: McGraw Hill, 1963).

Miller, Seymour M., and Roby, Pamela, *The Future of Inequality* (New York: Basic Books, 1970).

Mills, C. Wright, *The Power Elite* (New York: Oxford, 1967).

Mittelberg, Ekkehart, *Wortschatz und Syntax der Bildzeitung* (Marburg: Ewert, 1967).

Mosteller, Frederick, and Moynihan, Daniel P., eds., *On Equality of Educational Opportunity* (New York: Random House, 1972).

Negt, Oskar, *Soziologische Phantasie und Exemplarisches Lernen: Zur Theorie de Arbeiterbildung* (Frankfurt: Europäische Verlagsanstalt, 1968).

Neumann, Franz, *The Democratic and the Authoritarian State* (New York: Free Press, 1957).

Offe, Claus, *Strukturprobleme des Kapitalistischen Staates* (Frankfurt: Suhrkamp, 1972).

Parsons, Talcott, *The Social System* (New York: Free Press, 1951).

Partridge, Percy H., *Consent and Consensus* (New York: Praeger, 1971).

Peisert, Hansgert, *Soziale Lage und Bildungschancen in Deutschland* (Düsseldorf: Piper, 1967).

Piven, Frances F., and Cloward, Richard A., *Regulating the Poor* (New York: Pantheon, 1971).

Popitz, Heinrich et al., *Das Gesellschaftsbild des Arbeiters* (Tübingen: Mohr, 1967).

———, *Prozesse der Machtbildung* (Tübingen: Mohr, 1969).

Poulantzas, Nicos, *Pouvoir Politique et Classes Sociales* (Paris: Maspero, 1971).

Redford, Emmette S., *Democracy in the Administrative State* (New York: Oxford, 1969).

Rejai, Mostafa, ed., *End of Ideology?* (Chicago: Aldine, 1971).

Roig, Charles, *La Socialisation Politique des Enfants* (Paris: Armand Colin, 1968).

Runciman, Walter G., *Social Science and Political Theory* (Cambridge: Cambridge University Press, 1963).

Reich, Hans H., *Sprache und Politik* (München: Fink, 1968).

Roeder, Peter M. et al., *Sozialstatus und Schulerfolg* (Heidelberg: Quelle und Meyer, 1961).

Schramm, Wilbur, ed., *The Science of Human Communication* (New York: Basic Books, 1963).

Schumpeter, Joseph, *Capitalism, Socialism, and Democracy* (New York: Harper and Row, 1950).

Seidel, Eugen, and Seidel, Ingeborg, *Sprachwandel im Dritten Reich* (Halle, 1961).

Snow, Charles P., *The Two Cultures and A Second Look* (Cambridge: Cambridge University Press, 1965).

Touraine, Alain, *The Post Industrial Society* (New York: Random House, 1971).

Vygotsky, Lev S., *Thought and Language* (Cambridge: M.I.T. Press 1965).

Weber, Max, *Staatssoziologie* (Berlin: Duncker und Humblot, 1956).

———, *Economy and Society*, Guenther Roth and Claus Wittich, eds. (New York: Bedminster Press, 1968).

———, *The Protestant Ethic and the Spirit of Capitalism* (New York: Scribner, 1958).

Williams, Frederick, ed., *Language and Poverty* (Chicago: Markham, 1970).

Winckelmann, Johannes, *Legitimität und Legalität in Max Weber's Herrschaftssoziologie* (Tübingen: Mohr, 1952).

NAME INDEX

Name Index

Ladd, Everett C., 196n
Lafall, Julius, 14
Laing, Ronald D., 61
Larsen, O. N., 198n
Lawton, Dennis, 49, 50, 56
Lazarsfeld, Paul F., 197n
Lee, Susan P., 159
Lefebvre, Henri, 98
Lenin, V. I., 35
Lieberman, Jethro K., 205n
Lipset, Seymour M., 110, 135, 136, 143, 205n, 196n
Lipsky, Michael, 199n
Lispitz, L., 200n
Litt, E., 80
Loewenberg, Gerhard, 201n
Louis XVI, 129
Luckmann, Thomas, 186n
Luhmann, Niklas, 136–42, 165, 181
Luria, Aleksandr R., 17
Lyman, Elizabeth L., 117

Mallet, Serge, 200n
Mannheim, Karl, 103
Marcuse, Herbert, 3, 186n
Marx, Karl, 7, 19, 102–4, 116, 147
Mayntz, Renate, 101
McClosky, Herbert, 107, 200n
McCoy, Alfred, 196n
McKinley, Donald B., 66
McWilliams, Wilson C., 166
Medalia, N. Z., 198n
Merelman, Richard M., 136
Miliband, Ralph, 201n
Miller, Arthur H., 169
Miller, George A., 187n
Miller, Herman P., 199n
Miller, S. M., 199n
Mills, C. Wright, 4, 186n
Minuchin, Salvador, 61
Mittelberg, Eckehart, 98
Moore, Harriett, 116
More, Thomas, 83
Moser, Hugo, 36, 38, 39
Mosteller, F., 195n
Moynihan, Daniel P., 5, 81, 150, 195n
Musgrove, F., 66

Napoleon Bonaparte, 81, 131
Negt, Oscar, 199n

Newson, J., 193n
Newton, E., 185n
Nixon, Richard, 89, 112, 119, 123, 150, 196n

Oeverman, Ulrich, 195n
Offe, Claus, 184n, 197n, 201n
Olim, Ellis G., 17, 48
Orum, Anthony M., 193n
Orwell, George, 41

Paechter, Henry, 186n
Papon, Abbé, 202n
Parker, Richard, 199n
Parsons, Talcott, 136, 144–45, 154, 181
Patridge, Percy H., 93
Passel, Peter, 159
Passeron, Jean Claude, 194n
Peisert, H., 194n
Peters, Charles, 196n
Petkas, Peter, 204n
Pettigrew, T. F., 195n
Piaget, Jean, 15
Pischel, F., 185n
Piven, Frances, F., 184n
Powell, Lewis F., 89
Pressat, R., 195n
Prewitt, Kenneth, 66
Pritzwald, S., 40n

Queysanne, R., 196n

Reichwein, Regina, 51, 78
Reimer, E., 184n
Rejai, Mostafa, 106–7
Reznikow, L. O., 35
Riemschneider, E. J., 188n
Rinehart, James W., 114, 117
Rintels, David W., 99
Roby, P., 199n
Roeder, Peter M., 47
Roll, Charles W., 205n
Rose, Arnold, 4
Rosenzweig, M. R., 52
Rossi, E. J., 197n
Rothschild, Emma, 199n
Rousseau, Jean Jaques, 83
Rudikoff, Sonya, 152
Ruesh, Jürgen, 59
Rytina, Joan H., 200n

SUBJECT INDEX

Subject Index   223

Medical-industrial complex, 156
Meyers Lexicon, 26–28
Middle class, 128, 153, 179; anomie
in, 10; defined, 45; in deteriorated
social infrastructure, 159–60; education, 75, 77, 78, 80, 84–85,
190n; growth, 171; language, private, 71–72; language patterns and
structure, 11, 12, 45–58, 172;
loyalty, political, 6–7, 10; mothers,
48, 61–63, 65; occupations, 66–67;
parents and children, 48, 61–69,
172–73; political communication,
73; political symbols, 11; proletarization, 160; socialization, class-
specific, 58–73; taxes, 159; in
U.S., 10n; upper-, *see* Upper-middle class; values, 68–69, 148, 151,
154, 172; youth, 150, 181
Military expenditures, 121, 155–60,
162
Military-industrial complex, 155–60,
171
Minority, dominant, 112
Minority groups, 120; dissent and
protest, 6, 113; language problems,
18
Mobilization of bias, 92, 100
Monarchy, 129, 131; power of Louis
XVI, 129n
Moral principles, authority and, 132
Morrill Act (1862), 81
Mothers: black, 48, 61; middle-class,
48, 61–63, 65; upper-class, 65;
working-class, 61, 62
Motivation, defined, 133n

National Security Council, 90
Needs: articulation of, *see* Demands;
fulfilment of, 144–45; qualitative
or ideal, 9
"Newspeak," 41
New York *Daily News*, 98
New York Times, 98, 121, 124, 169
Noise (distortion), 95–97
Normative reorganization, 181
Normative predispositions, 111
Normative value, 109n
Norms, 109–10, 141; defined, 109n;
of industrial society, 154; transfer
from counterculture, 152

Open communication, 20, 138, 140,
181
Outer-direction, 65

Para-ideologies, 101, 108–12; of sci-
ence and technology, 109, 111,
112, 118, 135–36, 143, 180
Parents: authority, 62–63, 73; class-
specific values, 65–67; control of
children, 61–64, 73; political
values, 68–69; role structure, 73
Parliamentary government, 118
Parliamentary institutions, *see* Congress
Parties, political, 125, 160, 202n
Pentagon, 89n, 196n
Pentagon Papers, 90
Perception, language and, 16
Person-oriented behavior, 65, 73
Plausibility structure, 55
Pluralism, 4, 19, 103
Political communication, 18–42, 87–
92; constrained, 86–92, 133; lan-
guage as determinant of, 95–97;
legitimacy and, 133, 145; social
class and, 43–85; structural deter-
minants, 92–101; structured con-
sensus, 92–94; summary, table, 73;
symbols and, 71, 113
Political consciousness, 113, 160
Political integration, 4–6, 9–10, 108;
of working class, 108, 112–18
Political parties, 125, 160, 202n
Political phenomena, interpretation,
20
Political power, ideologies and, 108–
9; legitimacy of, *see* Legitimacy
Political socialization, 67–73; education and, 79–85
Political stability, 6–7; communication and, 84; language and, 19
Political symbols, 11, 71, 91, 113
Political system, 178–82; distrust of,
168–70
Political values, 11–12, 67–73
Politicization (politization): of ev-
eryday life, 160–63, 170, 180, 181;
of human service sector, 175, 180;
of professionals and cultural strata,
177
Politics, language and, 18–24